The No Quitters Guide
to Crushing Real Estate Investing
and Building an Extraordinary Life

The
NO QUITTERS
GUIDE

TO CRUSHING REAL ESTATE INVESTING AND BUILDING AN EXTRAORDINARY LIFE

NATHAN BROOKS

NEW YORK

LONDON • NASHVILLE • MELBOURNE • VANCOUVER

The No Quitters Guide to Crushing Real Estate Investing and Building an Extraordinary Life

Published in New York, New York, by Morgan James Publishing. Morgan James is a trademark of Morgan James, LLC. www.MorganJamesPublishing.com

Proudly distributed by Ingram Publisher Services.

Morgan James BOGO™

A **FREE** ebook edition is available for you or a friend with the purchase of this print book.

CLEARLY SIGN YOUR NAME ABOVE

Instructions to claim your free ebook edition:
1. Visit MorganJamesBOGO.com
2. Sign your name CLEARLY in the space above
3. Complete the form and submit a photo of this entire page
4. You or your friend can download the ebook to your preferred device

ISBN 9781631959370 paperback
ISBN 9781631959387 ebook
Library of Congress Control Number:
2022935518

Cover Design by:
Chris Treccani
www.3dogcreative.net

Interior Design by:
Christopher Kirk
www.GFSstudio.com

Morgan James is a proud partner of Habitat for Humanity Peninsula and Greater Williamsburg. Partners in building since 2006.

Get involved today! Visit MorganJamesPublishing.com/giving-back

TABLE OF CONTENTS

FOREWORD

There are three important things to know about Nathan Brooks, the author of the book you're about to read.

First—he could literally kill you with his bare hands.

The man is a *beast*, but a special kind of beast—the kind forged through thousands of hours of deliberate practice. Whether fighting a bloody opponent in the octagon or silently stalking a white-tailed deer through a dark wood, this handsome, tall, bearded, and chiseled man among men is a *warrior* through and through. You definitely wouldn't want to face him in *The Hunger Games.*

Second, Nathan is a genius at business—not because of some innate ability handed down from the gods, nor from being raised in the knowledge of generational wealth creation. Nathan is a special kind of genius—a genius born through decades of experience and pain. He's studied it. He's lived it. He's *suffered* in it. He's seen incredible highs, crippling lows, and has the scars and medals to prove it.

And third, perhaps most surprising, Nathan is a *poet*. Not in the "roses are red" kind of poetry, nor in the sense that you would ever see him awkwardly reciting lines in front of a hipster crowd at your local third-wave coffee shop on open mic night. He's a poet in the way *Merriam-Webster* defines a poet: *a creative artist of great imaginative and expressive capabilities*. In other words: Nathan is a poet because he sees what most others don't and communicates it in a way few others can, as you are about to discover.

It's this third surprising fact about Nathan that should excite you, the reader, today. Nathan sees the world in a different spectrum of light than most. While most of the world sees success as a series of tactics and steps, Nathan sees success as a process of purification that the mind, body, and soul undergo throughout a life well lived. It's the little things that Nathan notices, and throughout the book, describes. It's how we respond to failure. It's how we see and understand wealth. It's how we define what success really looks like for each of us. It's what we do with the seconds that add to minutes that turn to hours that lead to a life.

Success is not a mystery that only some can solve. Wealth is not a surprise to those who obtain it. An extraordinary life is not only destined for those with luck or unusual ability. These things are simply *results*. But results *of what?* What's the input you need in order to get the output of success? That, my friends, is the beauty of this book. It's here. You could read a hundred books on business, real estate, and personal development . . . or you could just read this one from Nathan. He's really compressed the best, must-know, fluff-free, life-changing advice into this fun and easy-to-read book that is destined to make a dent on the world.

Throughout the book, Nathan is expertly able to weave a tapestry of humble wisdom, inspiring stories, and keen observations on the true nature of success with one aim: to help you live an extraordinary life that's one hundred percent yours. If you're looking for a book on the latest get-rich-shortcut, pick up another book, probably one from a late-night TV infomercial or a Facebook ad. If you are looking for a book that's going to give you "five easy steps" to the outcome you want, pick up a magazine at the grocery store with the fake celebrity gracing the cover. And if you're looking for a step-by-step, detail-by-detail, how-to manual on investing in real estate—pick up one of mine! ;) But, if you're looking to address the inner person, the warrior, genius, poet who is inside you, waiting to come out, read on!

But I'll warn you: the inner and outer journey this book will take you on is not for the weak. It takes courage and strength to become a "no quitter" and live the life you were meant to live. It takes patience to become the kind of man or woman your family needs you to be. It takes dedication, persistence, grit, hard work, and time to build the kind of wealth you've dreamed of. But let me assure you: It's there, for the taking. No one is in your way, save yourself and the limiting beliefs you've temporarily tattooed in your mind.

The iconic singer-songwriter Bob Dylan once quipped, "A man is a success if he gets up in the morning and gets to bed at night, and in between he does what he wants to do." That is my hope and prayer for you today. And that is the central theme of the book you are about to read. You *can* live an extraordinary life.

And my good friend Nathan (a true warrior, genius, poet!) will show you how.

To your success,

-Brandon Turner,
Real Estate Investor & Host of BiggerPockets Podcast
Maui, HI
November, 2021

CHAPTER 1

THE PROBLEM:
"IF ONLY I COULD CHANGE MY LIFE . . ."

For most of my adulthood, I've been obsessed with creating an incredible life for myself and my family through building my real estate business. I've sought not just a dramatically improved financial position but also a fundamentally different life philosophy than what I grew up with—one that's based on living all-out all the time. To change my financial picture, I sought every possible educational opportunity I thought might help, even if it was nontraditional. I believed that making a positive lasting change financially in my life could help me create a massive positive impact on the world. I've committed to transitioning my focus from creating a business to giving away my money to improve housing, health, and education for children now and in the future. However, this past year, I was confronted with cascading anxiety and pressure over one key question:

Had I failed in the last decade to create the life I wanted?

This question led to an overpowering wave of sadness and fear. Did I miss connecting with what I really wanted in life? Were my purposeful actions not leading to the outcome I truly desired? I believe we receive answers to the hardest questions we harbor in our deepest and darkest places because we are finally open to receiving them. In the midst of my worry and despair, I had a vision of what the root issue was. I realized that all along I had been asking myself the wrong question. A pang of fire in my chest and a sick feeling in my stomach confirmed my suspicions. My life's work to this point had been a mission built on looking and feeling successful instead of finding a deep and meaningful purpose that could result in true success in every area of my life.

By all appearances, I was successful, but I only had the material trappings of success. I owned my own thriving real estate business, spent time doing things I loved with my family, owned a beautiful estate home outside the city, and had the recognition of my peers in the real estate world. I was crushing it in real estate. I was an influencer in my niche. I was living a life most people would envy. People who knew me or knew of me thought, *he made it.* Yet, there I was suddenly filled with painful angst and frustration with myself. My entire direction in life was wildly off course, missing the most important question and all-important answer that should have been directing it.

Who am I at my core, and how am I calibrating my thoughts, dreams, and actions into the best family life, personal growth, and work in my daily experience?

The worst part of asking myself this question was the realization that I didn't have a clear answer. Not even close. I was incredibly pissed off at myself for missing it. All along I thought I had been solving the right problem directed by the right question. I thought I had been relentlessly intentional, but I hadn't been. It was just a decade down the drain, right? Not that I ever put pressure on myself.

For weeks, I suffered from an intense feeling of complete failure. But, thanks to dear friends and life coaches, I slowly made my way back to the surface. Once I could be present again with myself, I committed to solving what went wrong in my questions and my thinking. When I figured that out, I could then align my actions with creating and living in positive, sustainable, and lasting change. Just as important to me as learning this for myself, I now feel inspired and compelled to share my experience because I want to help you do the same.

Crushing real estate is *awesome*. But lining up the work with the life I've always deeply wanted to live is truly my highest calling, and I hope it will be the highest calling for you as well.

What This Book Means to Me

Right now, you might be second-guessing your decision to pick up this book. You may be asking, *What kind of book is this, anyway!* So let me answer that question directly. Yes, this is a real estate book. It is also a book forged in my own life journey, written to change the way you look at your life. I want to ensure that all of the years of work and insane effort you put into your business create the joy, fulfillment, and life you actually want to live. I am a real estate investor with over a decade of experience. I've transacted tens of millions of dollars in deals annually for years, and within a year or so of writing this book, I will top one thousand units of homes built or renovated in my career. I've made millions of dollars through the renovation, new construction, and rental companies my partner and I have built. After only our first few years in business, we made the Inc. 5000 list of the fastest-growing companies in the United States two years in a row. Make no mistake, real estate has fundamentally changed my life. That's the power of this incredible field I have come to know and love (in ways that many people in my industry don't or can't).

I wrote this book to transform the way you think about the work you do right now. It will show you how to envision and plan an amazing journey that will take you from where you are now to whatever you want your life to be in the future. All accomplished through an incredible real estate business of your own design. You might be wondering how that is possible—how you can connect the dots between the work you are doing right now, the business you run, and the life that you want to live. I'm here to show you not just how to crush it in real estate but how to make all those amazing parts and pieces of your life congruent, effective, and capable of producing the desired end result of the extraordinary life you want to live.

For some time now, the loudest voices in the real estate investing world have been shallow ones. They hawk a sexy life of hustling, grinding, and making obscene amounts of money while totally skewing what is truly important. I can tell you that if you try to look impressive by posting pictures of checks for large sums of money on Instagram—or brag about what you are doing or where you live or how amazing you are—you are probably pretty unhappy immediately afterward when you have to deal with the real you. Often, I've found that people I've known like this have a frighteningly low sense of self-worth. They lack realness, integrity, and purpose beyond indulging their own egos. They have mistakenly looked up to the wrong mentors and guides. This way of thinking about real estate and life is wrong, and if this is you, it's hurting you.

The mission of this book is to think critically and carefully about every dimension of building a successful real estate empire, so that it provides the deepest and fullest life for you. You must understand and prioritize everything it takes to live the extraordinary life you want. For me, that life is fullest only when it is brimming with real personal joy and satisfaction. That comes from building and cultivating amazing relationships and fully loving and appreciating ourselves for who we are, where we have been, and who we are becoming. It will take all of your effort and work, but the real estate business you build will ultimately allow you to do what you love to do with the people you love.

Missing the Mark That Really Counts

Over the past six years, I have grown what has become an eight-figure annual business. During that time, I ran through all the checks and reviews that I knew to evaluate my business and my life. I *thought* I was happy and fulfilled. I didn't care about who other people thought I should be or what I should do, but what I *wanted*. I'd sought to create an amazing life ever since I was a teenager, maybe even younger. I actively created a mental image of what I wanted my future life to look like. However, when the crisis came and I started to look deep into what my life really was, I saw that not only had I not created what I wanted, but I also wasn't being honest with myself.

What is your ultimate purpose in wanting to live an extraordinary life?

This insanely powerful question was at the heart of a serious full-life review to finally find out what I did really want and why I was here. Despite everything awesome and positive I had accomplished, like building my business and watching my beautiful kids grow into the amazing people they are and are becoming, I still felt a lack of purpose. What was I on the planet to do? How could I have worked so hard on every other area of my life—my personal growth, my business—without pinning down that answer.

When it was apparent that this was a critical missing piece, it was impossible for me not to dig in. The self-examination was often painful, but I had to discover why I was off the mark and then decide what I needed to do about it. Only by working through many layers could I understand what was driving my emotions, my behavior, and my actions. I began to recognize patterns in my thought and decisions that had led me away from my purpose. I needed to consciously guide my thought and decision-making process, establishing new patterns that would bring my actions into alignment with why I was put on this planet.

As I took ownership of previous decisions, I still had moments when the old thought patterns would just pop up like an unwelcome guest in my brain and take over. I felt frustration that I didn't recognize the influence of other people's negative outlook or energy on me sooner. There was a voice saying I should feel guilt that I had allowed others' opinions to guide me instead of my vision. Then to avoid those emotions, I would move my focus outward on opportunities and ideas that I could chase in business or in fun hobbies. I had not turned light and energy back in on myself and asked, *Is everything you are doing congruent with the life you really want to live and the person you feel called to be?*

Unequivocally, in so many areas of life, it was not. This included my real estate business. Because I had wandered without focus and gotten into so many different ventures, nothing was really working. I found myself living in the space of others' negativity. I let my friends, relatives', and work associates' uncertainty, complaints and disappointments soak up my time and color how I felt. Instead of digging deeper into myself, my family, and my team to uncover issues, I would further compound them by trying new businesses or ideas, thinking that would be a solution. I didn't take into account the significant cost on our already taxed team as they tried to solve or integrate new ideas. Or whether those ideas were any good. The internal performance of our business and the personal satisfaction of our team didn't match the beautiful, finely molded exterior of our brand.

I started to realize that I had to first be present with my thoughts and ideas and gut-check whether they were actually what I wanted. I had to ask, *Who am I? What is our business for? How is it serving me and my family?* And only when I could answer those questions did I have full authority to live my best life. I would not let other people's negativity detract from my passion to become fully myself, or to impact my happiness or daily experience. I decided I would no longer allow the feelings, emotions, and desires of anyone in my life to impact what I knew was true for me or what I wanted. My focus from that day forward would only be on creating an incredible experience through meaningful relationships, fulfillment in every aspect of life, and enough income to have the financial resources to do the things I wanted to do. Life changed dramatically when I realized that everything I did was my choice and no one else's. It changed when I vowed to do everything in my power to live an extraordinary life.

So, I ask you, *Are you living an extraordinary life? Are you fulfilled in every aspect of what you do? Do you experience joy every day?* If you answered yes—although I've found that to be incredibly rare—this book is still for you because we are on the same journey together in discovering how we should live.

If you said no, but you deeply want a life of real purpose while also crushing it in real estate, this is your opportunity to create fundamental and meaningful change in your life so that you can live beyond your wildest dreams.

This is not your average real estate book. I won't regurgitate the basics of how to build a real estate business and what tools to use. There are hundreds of books that do that and many that helpfully outline the strategy and operations of the business you want to be in. Instead, this book will require you to dig deep and wrestle with hard questions about what you want in your life and how you might decide to get there.

No Success, Fame, or Money Is Worth Your Life

No matter how incredible your job, your business, or the size of your lucky family's fortune, you can't buy time with it. It's just not possible. Living the life you are truly called to live will mean you need to make the space—the time—to actually live it. Most people acknowledge there is a great distance between what they feel in their current daily experience and true happiness. But they lack the vision and understanding it takes to get out of the hole they are in. It's crushing. For years, we were told to get good grades, go to college, find a great job and hope that we could eventually retire to a life of leisure—a life that we couldn't really comprehend because it was so far in the future.

As we enter the workforce after our high school or college years, we are typically profoundly optimistic. We think that we can figure out how to add just a little bit more to our lives—in income, time, or fun. But soon the electric bills, rent, mortgage payments, and relationships draw us increasingly away from exploration that develops our unique identities. We feel the pull of a job because it provides this thing called *money*. And so it begins—the march of trading our precious life for money.

We hardly register that commonplace decision to take a job, but it leads to years of seeking work that has value or makes us feel valuable, accepted, and an important part of the team. All of a sudden, we may realize we aren't going to find a job like that (or that we aren't unemployable, as I did) and start trying to create work that we have some control over—that we can shape ourselves.

There's nothing wrong with any of this. Having an amazing job. Creating an incredible business. Being inspired and driven to accomplish something incredible. None of it is inherently bad. It's actually amazing when you think you've chosen to give your *life* to some cause or passion that's so important to you it's worth the investment. But how many times do we thoughtlessly make decisions without weighing the impact—on our families, our personal satisfaction, and the extraordinary life we were put on the planet to live.

Blink. You've woken up, just another day, and you've realized that you watched a decade or even more of your life literally sold to the highest per-hour bidder. Maybe it's the best possible sales position you could find, or a job that made you feel safe, or maybe just a job that took you away from whatever else was happening in your life. Maybe it's all you could do to just show up.

Is that really the life you want to live? I can't imagine it is if you picked up this book. It sure wasn't the life I wanted and living it put me in a constant state of wondering what could have been, while I was finding so little joy in the present.

You are not going to stay in that unfulfilling state. You are going to put into alignment, once and for all, how you spend your time, how you can create an amazing work life, and how you can grow your income so that it allows you to transform the way you live every day. Making money is awesome, and we are going to spend a lot of time on that. But so is finding the path that brings you incredible satisfaction doing the work you actually want to do. Don't be a slave to the notion that you need to put off being happy. Don't put off the vacation, dipping your toes in the sand and hearing the calm and soothing ocean waves. You can experience life now and every minute going forward because you'll have the financial resources and freedom they give. You will have mental space and time instead of being tied to work that consumes them. Why? Because you created, planned, and executed the steps that will change your life forever through investing in real estate.

I vividly remember taking a job as a mortgage originator in my mid-twenties. The recruiter told me about the massive amounts of money I would earn and how proud of myself I would be as a result. What he didn't even hint at was, well, everything else. How soul crushing it was to sit in one of hundreds of cubicles on the twentieth floor of a huge office complex. Basically, my thankless job was to pick up the hard black handle of the well-worn telephone at my desk and make calls over and over to people who mostly didn't want to talk to me. I'd look at the endless lists of names, addresses, and telephone numbers and dial yet another one, praying I would hear a friendly "hello" on the other end. But usually, I heard how much I had interrupted the person's day and that they had zero interest in refinancing their mortgage with me. The job was horrible.

Within just a few months, I knew this job would give me nothing that I'd hoped for. I had enough of the calls. I also didn't have much more in my nearly empty bank account. At a deeper level, frustration set in that came from working a job that I thought would create both incredible income and joy, but in fact, gave me neither.

Back to the Drawing Board. Again.

As I sit here writing this book, thinking of how you are experiencing this first chapter, life looks very different to me than it did back then. To be clear, it's not perfect. I am still working on many of the things I've talked about. Trying to bring my full self to every experience and opportunity. Finding and living in deep satisfaction and love in every moment of my everyday life. Believe me, I am not perfect at any of this. I've just chosen to work at becoming better. Staying relentlessly open to where my faults and weaknesses are. But with all this learning, my business has now grown to a place where it consistently generates income every month without my having to do much. This gives me vast amounts of time to experience life. I put in the work to create a business that serves me. And in turn I serve the team who work with me, who are going after their work with purpose because that's how the business was designed.

I'm finding that a perfect life isn't really about making a ton of money or having fancy things. It isn't about relishing constant attention or needing others to acknowledge who you are and what you've done. Success is actually about creating the time to live quietly inside yourself. Having the resources to do what you want to do every day. Living with a purpose and joy that feeds others who you want to be around, and live, interact, and grow with. When I meet people with tired and uninspired energy—people who aren't truly present, who aren't expecting great outcomes for themselves or others, or who are mired in complaining about things they make no effort to change—I have the confidence in who I am and what my life is about to shrug off their comments or attitudes. They make zero impact on me other than feeling that the love and peace I have is the opposite of their experience of life. What a different place I'm in to feel totally and fully myself while living the most extraordinary life. You can create whatever you want for yourself, too, and you are the only one who can.

If you are content with your situation in every way, then there may be nothing more for you to do. That's incredible! Enjoy your life. But if you are having less than the best experience of your life every day, then it's time to take a deep and serious look at where you have been and who you have become. What have you been thinking about during those precious moments that you have to yourself? There is an amazing person inside of you. Let's free that person and transform you into who you want to become, living the life you want to have.

The only thing in the way is you. Your negative self-talk. Terror and fear of a future that is unknown. Trauma in life that has hurt you, made you afraid to truly become the person you are called to be. Tap into that fear, that anxiety, that less-than-optimal, self-sabotaging belief. It's time you name it, claim it as a part of you, and consciously decide that from today forward, your intention is to create a life that you have designed, and every day you are worth living it.

CHAPTER 2

THE PROBLEM:
ARE YOU DOING SOMETHING THAT YOU LOVE?

I walked down the winding gangway and onto the 737 headed from Denver to Kansas City with anxious anticipation. I found my usual first-class aisle seat at the front of the plane and slumped into it, exhausted mentally and physically after another insanely grueling trip. For the past four days, I'd been in a deep dive with my business partner evaluating both the big-picture and operational planning of our real estate business. We had flown into Denver just days earlier for a gathering of some of the best real estate minds in the country. This group was made up of the who's who in real estate, all there to learn the secret tactics of the best companies in the country, and we were a part of it.

We always rolled into these meetings with a few specific problems we wanted to work on. Dialing in our acquisition strategies and numbers to track, and leading and growing our team were two of them. But on this trip, there was a fire inside of me. At the time, I hated everything about my real estate business.

It didn't matter that our business was successful. I didn't even want to walk through the front door of my own office building to deal with the team I had hired to operate our business. I couldn't see any way to change the culture, the people, or the leadership. And most soul-crushing of all was the realization that it was all my fault.

I had been working like crazy, my family relationships weren't great, I wasn't spending time with the people I loved or doing things that excited me. I micromanaged at work, unable to allow people to be great at what they do. I thought I had to see every issue, direct every move, and come up with every idea. I was unhappy and not sure how to fix any of it.

Creating a real estate business that serves your life is an incredible aspiration. It's also a challenging journey. The dreaming and envisioning of what I could create was the easy part for me. I could paint a beautiful mental picture of what I wanted my life to be. Where I would live. What car I would drive. The kinds of vacations I would take. And the biggest dream of all— financial freedom. No more worrying about the credit card bill or the cost of the kids' activities. I wanted to take on much better problems than these, like how to create an even more amazing business and how to spend more quality time with my family and friends.

You can curate an amazing life for yourself. It's not complex in spirit, but it takes serious thought and work to create what you truly want. It also takes serious perseverance and discipline to hold onto your vision and resist going after the exciting or shiny objects in the moment.

The problem in these potential transformational moments is that we don't allow ourselves to believe we can create the life we really want. We look down on our ability and deny our capacity. We cultivate self-doubt instead of self-belief. Of course, you can't be successful with that mindset. It's not possible. You've already decided that you will fail before you've even started.

Initially, my mental block to success was a complete disconnect between what I wanted my business to look like and *why* it was built that way. What was I actually building this business to *do* in my life? How many hours would I be working? What was my job and the everyday responsibilities I needed to accomplish? Then, how do I get from inception to actually seeing my ideas manifested in a real business and life experience.

Ask yourself these questions: What does not feel fulfilling in your current daily experience? Is it the people you're around? The work that you do? How do you feel while doing it? What is incongruent now with the life that you want to lead? Your answers will make it easier to connect to what you want as you begin to paint a picture of what your future life and experience should look like. Make your plan so detailed and clear that you can't help but play that movie in your mind.

Without the trinity of a clear vision, the strategy to get there, and the concrete steps to take to make it happen, there is no plan. And there is no business. And then there is no extraordinary life.

Start with a Clear Picture

I vividly remember living in the first home that my wife and I bought together and thinking, *If only I could make $6K a month, life would be amazing.* At the time, my wife was changing little kids' lives as a teacher at a nearby elementary school, and I was working during the day slinging guitars at a local music shop. I was playing out three or four nights a week as a professional musician too. Thinking back now, it's almost hard to believe that $6K was my target and that I hadn't set my sights much higher. You will learn as we get further into the book that the bigger goals you set are actually easier to hit than the smaller ones. I also acknowledge that right now it may seem like a huge stretch for you to make even $5K or $10K a month, just like it did for me.

We were basically broke all the time, and being broke is hard. It's life-draining. I'd constantly dream of a week where we could eat out a few times, pay our bills without worry, and not have another complete breakdown at the end of the month when once again we had charged too much money on the credit card. We were always trying to find a way to pay what we'd put on it, and we'd start the next month once again in the hole.

I loved playing music for a living, but between making time for practice, working at the guitar shop, and booking and playing shows, it basically took up my entire life. There wasn't any time for the family, vacations, or just having the space in normal life to chill out and reset. I was working a job that I didn't love and wasn't supporting the life I wanted to live.

Earning a high income is not a stretch goal. It's not a joke or a misguided dream. To me, it is an imperative piece of a life well lived. Financial resources are tools that let you do the things and live the life that you want. But first you must believe that it is actually possible to achieve. This is the starting line on the path to a new reality and mindset about what you do for work and why, and how you are financially compensated for your time, effort, and ideas. So often, the problem lies not in your dreams or opportunities but in the degree of self-belief you have.

As you cultivate ideas of what you want your life, your income, and your daily experience to be, you may become excited about the possibilities. Your ideas might start to seem more real. Your head can feel like a shaken soda can, ready to burst with ideas to share with others. But there's a catch at this exhilarating moment. Unless your core group of friends and family have either solved similar problems or are totally supportive of you in this new mission, they will likely be of no help. They may even be a negative distraction as you seek to accomplish what you want. Just remember you get to decide if acting on your dreams and goals is worth it to you or if you are willing to let someone else deny the outcome of your life

The fact is, you can create a business that serves you. But you have to decide if you want it bad enough to deal with those friends and family with their strong opinions. And if you want it bad enough, seek out support elsewhere, for example from creditable coaches and mentors. Who you ask for help makes a dramatic difference.

Not only have I come close to accomplishing the kind of space and experience in my life that I want; I have many friends, colleagues, and coaching students who have too. One of my students worked for the railroad. He'd worked hard for years and liked what he did, but was also tired of the rat race of working for a company rather than having his own business that would allow him the opportunity to make his own decisions.

Over the course of several years, he built a small real estate portfolio by investing in apartment syndications that paid out great returns each quarter. With clarity and diligence, he played the long game, pacing himself by buying only a few homes each year as he continued to work for the railroad. Over time he was able to build a multimillion-dollar net worth. Today he owns millions in real estate, has retired from his job, and travels regularly all over the world doing amazing things with his family.

He can do it. I can do it. **You can do it.** You only need to make a decision based on your answers to two questions: How bad do you want it? And what are you willing to do to accomplish what you really want in life?

The Life-Sucking Feeling That Won't Go Away

The initial thought we often have when we take stock of our lives is *I want to make a little more money.* Right? You want to be able to live a good life. Be happy. Take your two weeks of vacation and get to the beach. Pick up a few extras at the grocery store for the weekend instead of sticking to the "must-haves" on the shopping list. Play the familiar tune of "I can't even pay for basic living expenses right now, so how could I possibly have the money to invest in real estate?" I have lived there a lot, often with no connection back to the action I had to take. Also not helpful.

I would imagine something incredible I wanted to accomplish, but I'd find myself descending from the mental high altitude of the idea to the soul-sucking realization of my current situation. My dream wasn't really my life. Not even close. And there was so much distance, work, and learning between where I was in my life and where I wanted to be. The powerful feeling of possibility so quickly became a nightmare of self-doubt, taunting me: *I bet you couldn't do it anyway.*

I've heard these kinds of negative comments so many times I want to ban them from common conversation and all internal dialogues. Does this dream-killing conversation sound familiar? You say, "I can just deal with this job I hate; it's not that bad. At least I have a job, I guess." Then, usually with the best intentions, a friend or family member says, "Yeah, real estate was a pretty cool idea. But maybe it's just not for you. You don't know much about real estate anyway, right? It was going to be a failure from the beginning." You take what people say to heart and start to think they're right.

In case you were wondering, these negative responses are really terrible things to say to anyone, but most especially to your beautiful self. There is nothing helpful, inspirational, or tactical that will come from such self-criticizing thoughts. And that harsh language you use and defeated story you tell yourself is one-hundred percent trash. You choose what you tell yourself and what you believe. It's my personal belief we are always our own biggest obstacle. No matter what excuse you use, it's yourself, your mindset, and your willingness to dig into the long journey of creating serious, lasting, and amazing change. The key is not succumbing to the impulse to give up because then you are guaranteed not to accomplish what you want.

What really used to upset me, though, was the mental pendulum. My thoughts would swing from my incredible dreams to self-criticism, again and again. It felt like an inescapable loop of excitement over the possibility, then self-doubt, self-criticism, and disbelief over whether I was capable of accomplishing the goals I'd set out. It's so easy to get stuck between what you know and understand and what you think is out of reach but is so ripe with the potential to transform your life.

To get unstuck, you have to ask yourself, what is living an extraordinary life ultimately worth? To me, it was worth having to get past the fear of failure and past the fear of what others thought of me, although that is still something I am working on. It's a real possibility that you could put all this effort into your dream, and it still doesn't work out. Many people before us have made this entrepreneurial journey, so we know that it *can* work. Deep down, have you really decided that you are committed to it working, and will you do absolutely everything, including failing time and time again, to accomplish what you want? *That* is the question we all have to answer.

You Are Going to Do *Something* with Your Time

Regardless of whether you decide to pursue your dreams or let them continue to fester as untried fantasy, you are going to do *something* with your time. That is, while you are still alive and breathing, you are choosing how you spend your time. Take a moment to look down at yourself and see every detail—really see yourself from above, not from inside your head. You are the observer of you, and in this moment, you can watch whatever decision you make in your life and how it looks as if you were watching a movie.

First, visualize you decide going after a real estate business is just not worth it. You've decided it's too scary. You don't have enough money, skills, or experience. You can't do it. Working that hard or that long is just not worth the outcome. Although all of these challenging roadblocks are removable, you've decided to quit on yourself. There you are, stuck working that dead-end job, not experiencing an amazing daily existence. You're barely getting by. The money is just above tolerable, and the people you work with, including your boss, pretty much hate their jobs too. Every minute at work is another reminder that you *quit* on yourself.

By the time you get home at night from your life-sucking endeavor, you're so drained mentally, emotionally, and maybe even physically, you are an empty shell. Missing more opportunities for connection, fun, and joy with your family and friends, you sit in front of the television or lose another hour of your life on some social media platform. You make some food, complete the necessary bedtime routines, and lay your head on the pillow.

How does living that life feel to you? I feel a little sick reading back through how that life was for me. A few feelings show up too: miserable, heartbreaking, unfulfilled, broken, sad, unhappy. Life is so precious, and every one of us has serious human value. We are here to find our place in the world, live an amazing life, and be fully who we are called to be as valuable people. Know that we all have the choice to do whatever in the world we want to do. Why would anyone choose a life they don't love living?

Now look down at yourself making the decision to go after what you want. No matter what, you are committed to being successful at creating a different life. The timeline is unclear. The path to get there is winding and will include many lessons, challenges, and frustrations, but that is what you sign up for when you want to live an extraordinary life. You see yourself first creating an incredible vision of what you want your life to look like. You think about what part of your work you most enjoy. Sometimes you will have to do activities or jobs that you don't like on this path, but you can identify those things and work over time to find someone who does love doing them. A win for you and a win for them.

You might feel at first that your plan is moving and business is growing at an incredibly slow pace. You might even worry at times that you have made the wrong decision. For example, a deal you really needed to make for this month's income doesn't close and you have to figure out what to do. Or there was a series of decisions that you made a few months ago that today you discover didn't lead you where you really wanted to go. You must look back at what happened, what needs to change, and make a different decision going forward. Changing direction is a normal and expected part of the journey. Because this is your life, your plan, and your goals, you get to make the changes that need to be made.

A year flies by because your goals and the new opportunities are now your most important focus. This new business not only changes your work experience but impacts every area of your life. It affects your family connection, your financial capacity, and your decision-making abilities. You now make decisions based on what you want to do rather than allowing your current circumstances to limit you. You gain a new willingness to learn and to grow in new environments. Watch yourself stretch into this new amazing you.

At the start, the business barely makes any money. You are just scraping by in everything you are doing, but also learning and adjusting at hyper speed. You begin to find your footing. Your decisions open a clearer path, connected to your end goal because you have spent so much time solving problems and seeing opportunities that lie ahead. You now see where others can join you and be a part of your dream. You empower them to help you solve problems and do work they love. You scale and build your life with others who share the same vision. Your time begins to free up. You have more capacity for living life and are making more money than you ever thought possible, allowing you to do things you really enjoy.

So this is your crossroads. Making the decision to not go for what you really want means your dream isn't important enough to you. It's not exciting enough. Or it isn't what you want after all. Or worse, you don't care enough in the end to make a change. You'd rather complain and make excuses than adjust your course and do something different. The secret is to envision a future so insanely exciting, motivating, and life-giving that you can't *not* take action right now. Your everyday routine in its current form is life-sucking, and it has to change today. But even if you haven't formulated the vision of what your life might look like clearly enough to take the first step today, you can still start to dream and mold your plan.

If you decide that you're in, then you are accepting the responsibility to do everything in your power to manifest this new vision of your life. It may surprise you to know I've worked many more insanely difficult and frustrating days in my own business than I have worked for someone else. Honestly, it's not even close. How badly did you want this change again? To me, the hard work didn't matter. The more issues came up, the more invested and motivated I was to learn whatever was needed, to look critically at the problem in a different light, to change or develop a solution, or to ask someone else to help determine what was really needed. Never once will you hear me say this is an "easy" journey. People who say that haven't done the work. Don't listen to them.

The path becomes clearer and clearer as you travel down it toward your desired destination, which is finally within sight. The effort on this last leg of the journey is worth it. Every day, every opportunity, every challenge is just a series of decisions and a choice. Am I going to solve this today and accomplish what I really want, or am I going to *quit?*

I've spoken over and over with new investors, working through their first steps, first trials, and first questions about their own real estate investing journey. Invariably, I hear, "I love what you are doing. Can I come work for you? I wish I was there." It's almost like it's too good to be true from where they are sitting when they look at what I've accomplished. They see somehow I was able to figure it out but fear they aren't smart enough to figure it out for themselves. Believe me, I am far from the smartest person in the room. I just won't quit.

Maybe your block to action is being afraid of all the work that has to go into creating a new business. If so, that chaos-creating fear is rooted in being unsure of yourself and if all the work will produce what you want. Keep pushing yourself past the fear of the unknown toward the end result you envision.

Every single day, every one of us makes decisions. To be happy. To live an amazing life. To figure out how to go on that vacation you always wanted or to go to college. So what if you haven't made the same decision in the past to make massive change? Today, you get to make a different decision. Maybe you're at a crossroads that forces you to make a change in your life. Maybe you've hit the limit of what you *don't* want your life to be. You could be floundering, waiting, and wishing for some additional inspiration to make a change. Or just terrified altogether. No matter where you are, be honest with yourself, and be present with what you want your life to look like. You get to start from where you are now, and that is okay.

Regardless of what you decide, one thing is true: Your life is not someone else's decision. Not someone else's problem. You are not stuck or unable to make a change because of some outside force. This was a story running inside of me for a long time. I let my view of how I thought others saw me run wild, affecting every area of my life. Ask yourself truly: How bad do I want this new life that I say I want? And what am I willing to do about it? No more negative stories and no more self-doubt. Your life is yours alone to create. Hold yourself to that responsibility. Each of us can create the life we want, and it is solely up to us to take action.

CHAPTER 3

REAL ESTATE DONE WRONG

I had a window seat to many poorly laid and executed plans during the Great Recession in the early 2000s. At the time, I was working as a real estate agent and investor, putting together exit plans for people in financial straits. My job was to help them get out of the house they needed to live in but couldn't afford, move somewhere they didn't want to live, and find money they didn't have for the new place. I would sit in their kitchens, watching them panic with tears in their eyes, and work through how best to sell their house and not lose their dignity in the process.

Over and over, I felt a deep gratitude that I was not having to go through that awful experience. Even though the conditions that created these crises were so clear and present, I believed I would never end up there myself. Nearly everyone I worked with had either lost a job or was making significantly less income than they were before. Most people didn't have much in savings and quickly went in the hole with no money and very few options.

That experience working through the middle of the housing foreclosure crisis returned to haunt me in the latter part of 2009. Although I was then successfully transacting millions of dollars of sales as a real estate investor and agent in Florida, I was still dealing with poor decisions I made years before when I started my real estate portfolio in Kansas City. Not only had my initial plan of building that real estate portfolio been vague at best; my operation and management strategies were incomplete and incoherent. I hadn't been prepared when I started. I didn't have enough money, I borrowed from a bank that did not act ethically, and I bought houses that needed more work than I was prepared to take on. I had no knowledge of renovation or construction, and no idea how to manage tenants. All of these problems had snowballed. My situation was quickly sliding from the dream of dramatically changing my life to utter chaos. I found myself in the same desperate and dark place as all those clients I had helped. I was broke, terrified, and afflicted by a feeling of complete helplessness and deep embarrassment over what to do about my impossible circumstances. I feared I would lose everything.

I vividly remember thinking, *How did I end up here, too? I should have known better. I should have seen it coming.* Regardless, I was financially and emotionally broken from my poor personal financial management along with numerous unforeseen and costly maintenance and tenant issues. Being unable to pay the mortgages on the rental homes I owned didn't change my obligation to pay them. I couldn't hold those obligations any longer.

After examining every possible option, every way out of my situation other than legal help, I saw I'd reached a dead end. I always prided myself on figuring out workable solutions to any problem, but this one I just couldn't solve. Completely panicked, I reached out to my friend and real estate attorney for help. This was the person who helped me put together deals in Florida and now I had to tell him I was sinking in Kansas City. He tried to work through the problem with me, but no matter what he said, I knew where I was headed.

In December 2009, my wife and I filed for Chapter Seven bankruptcy. Gone was my feeling of worth, my strength as a man, and my confidence that I could provide for my family.

Filing for bankruptcy is actually not that hard to do. After my wife and I answered what seemed like hundreds of detailed questions about our financial status—the houses we owned, the cars we drove, and the debt we had—filing was a matter of paying a few thousand dollars and signing documents. Yet I had little understanding or appreciation for the decade it would take to mentally work through my failures or the financial and banking complications of carrying the scarlet letter B—for Bankrupt.

Once we filed for bankruptcy, there was some initial relief from the bills we couldn't pay and from being overwhelmed by the situation. The banks and credit card companies stopped calling us. But soon the date of our hearing arrived, and there we were, anxiously driving to the massive city building that housed the trustee overseeing our case. Her responsibility was to figure out what assets we had and use them to pay back the debts we owed.

We found our way to the upper levels of the towering building and wound our way through the halls to the courtroom where our hearing was scheduled. As we entered the room, it was as if there was an energy vacuum. Everyone inside was broken and scared, and we were among the weary, clueless as to what was going to happen.

Get Rich Schemes Are Broken

Being inspired to make an incredible living is an awesome feeling, and it can give you the momentum to make changes and create what you really want in your life. However, there are many financial gurus in the world who prey on people, charging insane amounts of money for programs that are lackluster at best. They market and advertise their services by boasting about how easily they made their millions. All you have to do is give them your credit card and pay them to share how they did it. There are great programs and mentors out there, but you have to find a mentor or coach who is aligned with what you want and will help guide you while also looking out for your interests.

Building wealth starts with an objective beyond the money. It absolutely must. Assess what your life really looks like instead of focusing only on the insatiable quest for a dollar or for the next shiny thing. Please understand that making money, even a lot of money, is awesome. Money is a tool, and we can use it to take amazing journeys, live in a rock-star palace, or change the world. The more of it we have, the bigger the tool and the more leverage we have. However, all of the wealthiest people I know didn't become wealthy fast. Their journey wasn't a perfect linear line without bumps, bruises, or runarounds. Plenty of times they had to stop and figure out where they had been or where they were going. The growth of their businesses and their wealth happened over time as they learned and applied lessons by making changes that positively impacted the end result.

My friends who are worth millions or tens of millions of dollars have experienced the cycle of learning, innovating, and adapting for many years. There was no "get rich" scheme. No perfect formula or experience. Each of their journeys was a little different but had one common denominator. They had to work diligently and effectively over time while creating and maintaining an insanely clear vision attached to a big why. Nearly all worked to create a team able to help them with a blend of both patience and persistence to accomplish what they wanted.

Do you really want to be wealthy? Then keep the focus on where it should be—the *why* behind what you are doing. And then focus on the plan to get you there. Money may come, even with poorly laid plans. But can you imagine working for the next ten years growing a real estate business only to look back and hate everything you built? Your life-changing business will take time, so build one that you will love being a part of and committed to for the long run.

You Don't Need a Massive Social Media Following

Opening up your favorite social media accounts and seeing hundreds of thousands of followers might sound exciting, but it actually doesn't mean anything. Building an amazing life through real estate doesn't have anything to do with a need for attention. Showing off the sushi place where you just dined or trying to post the best-liked pictures of yourself is just a distraction. Nearly every person I know who is obsessed with how they are perceived by others, instead of being grounded in the calling and the work they are supposed to do, is miserable and sad. This isn't *The No Quitters' Guide to Make a Lot of Money but Be Miserable*. Even in a society where everyone values and craves attention and constant personal reinforcement, we each get to make a decision about how we use social media. Is all that effort constantly putting together pictures, videos, blogs, and stories really worth it?

I do know several amazing investors who have a large social media presence, including my friend Brandon Turner, Bigger-Pockets podcast co-host, author, and real estate investor. The inspiration behind his drive in life wasn't to have all these people follow him but to do what he loved in real estate—talk about it and help others follow his example. I'd say it worked out pretty well for him because he is now raising tens of millions of dollars for massive real estate deals in a matter of days, crushing it with a large portfolio of extremely successful books and kicking it with his amazing family in Hawaii. His social media success grew over time, and it wasn't what made him wealthy at first. And it sure didn't bring him as much fulfillment as his mission to help others, carve out more family time, and enjoy more freedom.

You might want to help a larger audience change their lives through real estate, and you can do it using social media. I am down with that. Just don't kid yourself into believing that using social media to shine a giant light on yourself will give you what you really want. Creating a business, philosophy, and mission that serves you is awesome. Then you can invite others in as you are able to give value and share insights on how to change lives, using any media you like.

Perpetual Hustle and Grind Is a Broken Mindset

In today's culture, the hustle and grind is often seen as sexy, but it's a sadistic, work-yourself-to-death rite of passage. You can tell everyone how hard you work and how important you are to the mission and the success of a company, but the problem is that you can literally "grind" yourself into the earth or at least into misery. How about I save you some time by telling you to just not do that? You can't live an amazing life if you work yourself to death.

On your journey, there will be many challenging times when you will be required to do tremendous work. The most difficult growth I've experienced came during the hardest challenges I've faced. Working one hundred hours a week forever is not a badge of honor; it is an effective path to self-destruction and misery. It's also not smart when you have a team. I've experienced this cycle of overworking and being overwhelmed more than I would like to admit. Sometimes I felt I needed to be in the middle of the problem I was solving. Sometimes I just found myself in the middle of a storm I didn't see coming. But on the other side of each of these experiences, I've realized that the more I worked over long periods, the less effective I was. I'd insert myself into the middle of the problems rather than allowing space and opportunity for those closest to the problem to solve it. Just because I am the owner of the business or the leader of the team, I came to realize, doesn't mean I should make all the decisions or that I even have the best answers.

Building anything of size and impact requires a serious amount of time, focus, and attention. But it's less burdensome if you remember you are not the only person who can carry your vision forward. Believing you must do it alone is a broken mindset and it's also insanely ineffective. It means you've built your business around your need to work and feel worth from it. Instead, create a vision that includes connecting and building amazing relationships with people who share your vision. This will allow you to focus on the work you love in your business and also allows others to be invested in the overall outcome. Your team can not only help you create an amazing life, but also create amazing lives for themselves too.

Money Isn't the Only Objective

Making money for me is a mental marathon. I love finding interesting opportunities and then solving the challenging puzzle of taking them from idea to actuality. This involves working with creative, smart people and building winning relationships with them. These relationships, by the way, are a fantastic resource in my life. Owning and working in real estate is not just about owning a lot of property or making a lot of money. Money doesn't create happiness, and it certainly doesn't solve mental, emotional, personal, or business problems. Money solves money problems. It seems intuitive for a lot of people that money will suddenly change their life, but it won't unless that life is built and curated with purpose.

I had this crazy realization making money created its own problems—namely, what to do with it once you make it. As I started to bring in more money, it was easy to spend frivolously rather than execute a plan for where that money was going to go. Imagine working hard to create an amazing business and then wasting all that hard-earned time and cash on something that doesn't really add to your life? No matter how much money you make, without a plan that you diligently execute, you will not get what you want.

Start first with a simple plan based on your monthly household budget. Be sure to include everything, such as your food, clothes, vehicles, utilities, and mortgage or rent. Without investing time in determining your budget, you won't know how much you have allocated to spend, save, invest, or give away. You are working and earning with no direction.

Next, decide how you want to invest your money. I start with a clear, big-picture plan before assigning any dollar amounts. In making my plan, I can ensure my strategy is scalable so as my business grows, I can increase the dollar amount of my investment and check if my plan still works. For instance, if your active business is holding rental houses, as your cash flow grows, you could either pay the houses down faster, buy more houses, or invest that money in something else entirely. If you have a lot of expenses for a month or two, you could decide not to pay extra down on them. Then you can just pick up your plan again once you covered those expenses. Having an incredible life means you thoughtfully account for every aspect, including how you will invest and grow your wealth over time.

Zero Focus = Lackluster Results

Creating a real estate business, or any business for that matter, means you also need to understand fundamentally what it is built to do. If you find yourself having a hard time figuring out what area of real estate to focus on, that's okay. Keep thinking, learning, and creating a plan. It will come together. When you are ready, pull the trigger and go after the one big idea, whatever it is.

Don't divide your attention. You and your team, who are also working toward this goal, can't have unclear and/or competing priorities. Every new idea you propose takes the focus off the one big idea that you should be hammering away at with all of your attention and your team's. Focus on the one thing you want to accomplish and commit.

In the future, you can certainly own many businesses or add different facets to your real estate empire. Start with one idea, grow it, and allow it to flourish into what it can be, and then it can begin to operate and function without you. Create and cultivate great leadership from the beginning and stay grounded in the plan you've laid out. Focused initiative with a worthy goal creates a winning combination for success.

I've had to learn this the hard way and am still learning it. I live for creating new opportunities and dreaming of how to put the pieces of new puzzles together in a beautiful way. But being a successful entrepreneur requires you move from dreaming many dreams to prioritizing one. Make the decision now you will honor the primary goal and objective you have set out to accomplish, because it will make your focus and your team's effort clear. As you have ideas, write them down in your journal and allow them time and space to develop and mature as ideas.

Don't assume that just because you thought of an idea, you have to take action on it. Your team will thank you.

If you still aren't sure about how to start, lay out what the options might be. Owning single-family rentals or storage units, even apartments, for example. What would you like about each of those? How would the decision to pursue one of those options affect the life you want to live? Also ask yourself what areas of the business you are personally excited to be responsible for. All of these questions will help define what kind of business you want to start and how that business and your work within it will impact the way you live your life.

My business must serve me as an owner. But it also must serve the clients I work for and their objectives, and the team I hire that runs everything. It is not possible to live an extraordinary life without having a really clear purpose for your life and lining up the activity in the business so that it's congruent with that purpose. If your clients are happy and what you do helps them, they will tell others and keep coming back. And serving and caring for your team will ensure they are happy, fulfilled in their work, and continue to help your business not just run but grow and thrive even without you in the middle of it.

Your one mission now is to create a business that is in alignment with your desired life. Period. Of course, you will make changes over time or need to pivot with the market or whatever you decide you want the next stage of your life or business to be. But take the time now to plant the seeds of what your incredible future life will look like. Evaluate your new and amazing ideas to see which one will be your focus. Then, transform that idea into clear plans and tactics that will move your vision from dream to reality.

Prepare Your Growth Mindset Now

Know that you are going to encounter challenges and frustrations along your journey, and that is okay. Prepare for them. When an issue comes up, it is just another opportunity in a series of opportunities to transform your business into the amazing machine it will become. And this allows you time to grow into the strong and thoughtful leader you need to be.

Don't shortcut your planning, your learning, or your effort. Put the first things first every time, planning and then implementing each aspect of your plan with the focus and preparation that they require. You will have opportunity after opportunity to lose focus, so prepare yourself for that, too. Convince yourself that no matter what, you will stay on task, understand what you are working toward, and get after it.

Building your new business and chasing what you want out of life is exciting, but it is also a long game. What you are building is the opposite of a "get rich" scheme, which don't ever really work. You are building an incredible business with a solid foundation. You will create it and determine how it will function. You will mold it, applying your ideas, and will manifest those ideas in real life. Creating and building my own business is both the most amazing work I've ever done and the absolute hardest. Over and over, I have realized that the clarity of my focus and my capacity to lead directly relate to the effectiveness, happiness, and success of my team.

Sometimes your decisions will be spot-on in leading you toward the goal you want to accomplish, and sometimes what you decide to do won't work at all. Someone you hire won't work out, and you have to fire them. A project will be delayed or a contractor will bail from the job. A house you plan to make money holding long term will have to be sold because things just didn't go well. Plan for the unexpected. Embrace that not everything you try is going to work, but that doesn't mean the overall objective or plan won't work.

Take a clear and honest approach in dealing with whatever happened, whatever decisions were made, and choose to try again. This time, take a different approach. Having your own business means you must create a team culture of identifying what the problems are, understanding them, and creatively solving them—as a team. Give everyone you work with the authority and responsibility to identify issues, even if the issue is you. You and your team will then have the trust and confidence to tackle any kind of problem and solve it in alignment with your goals because you set up your business to work that way.

Are you feeling a little twinge of fear that things won't work, and you won't know what to do? That is totally normal. Doing something new can lead us down the rabbit hole of self-doubt and even to scary thoughts of what awful things could happen. We can paint vivid, terrifying mental pictures of our business failing or finding ourselves in situations we don't know how to handle. Stop right now with the negative thoughts. Instead, as thoughts come up that create anxiety, identify what the actual issue is, attack what it is that is driving that anxious feeling, and create a solution.

View every single decision you make through the lens of how it will impact the purpose of your business. Will your choice help create the life you want? Will the team understand why the decision was made, and is it in alignment with your mission and strategy? Even if the idea is really cool, if you didn't answer a full-bodied yes to those questions, your decision is a no. We aren't doing anything in our business that doesn't serve us as the owners, the team we are asking to bring this idea to life, or our clients. I would have saved myself a lot of heartache and a serious amount of money if I had implemented this litmus test for what is important earlier in my business.

Don't Make Yourself the Most Important Person

Regardless of whether your name is on the building or your title is CEO, creating the business you want means building an amazing team around you to execute the mission. It's easy to believe that you are the best person to make every decision in every area of the business. But that kind of self-important thinking is a broken mindset and one that will only hamper your ability to grow and build the life and business that you really want.

Instead, encourage, mentor, and empower the team you hire to bring your real purpose to life. Communicate consistently what your big vision is. Once your team members understand and see your vision, they will want to be a part of making it happen. Accept that people are going to make mistakes, and let them know that's okay. You won't want them to make the same mistake over and over, of course, but it is part of learning and life to make the wrong decision sometimes.

Creating a culture of collaboration and conversation will help the team to review and discuss what the objectives are, how they relate to your company goals, and how to align and merge them. By having different kinds of people involved, you'll get different viewpoints about ideas or issues, which will help you make more thoughtful and complete decisions on how to move forward.

For a business to serve you, it has to be able to run without you. You can't do everything. It's not possible. If you try to be most important, you will wake up one day and hate what you are doing even if you are successful—just like I did. You'll realize that you are responsible for creating a business that's a burden to you instead of creating the space for others to come in and help you. What work you want to do day-to-day in the business will change over time. This is natural and will open up opportunity for someone else to come in to handle those responsibilities. They will bring fresh eyes and ideas to their new role, energizing your amazing company. Understand and embrace that. Because you can clearly articulate what the job is and how it relates to everything else in the company, having people move into new roles shouldn't be scary. Onboard and train every person you bring along for this business journey with the same positive intention and expectation. Everyone we work with has a passion for what they do, isn't afraid of challenges or hard work, and wants to learn and grow individually and as a team. As the owner, create the space and opportunity for every person you hire and work with to love the work they do. Give them full responsibility and the power to do the job you hired them to do.

Each hire or engagement with a new outside vendor will bring you closer and closer to having the freedom to choose what work you do in your business and to spend more time outside of it. Wasn't that part of your dream, not to be working every second? You've created a cool company with a clear vision of what it is and a killer team who want to go out and slay the world every day.

Failure to create that clear vision or a culture of collaboration or that well-trained and empowered team will mean problems. An undefined purpose doesn't provide a meaningful reason to work hard when challenges arise. A team that isn't led well and isn't trusted will look for a different work environment, so you will struggle with turnover. You'll be continually trying to find someone to do the work that you don't want to do. This leads to more frustration for you and the team, and you are stuck working in an area of the business you don't want to be in.

Don't let this be you. Create your business with a purpose that goes far beyond just making money for yourself. We all want to be a part of something awesome that is beyond ourselves. Ideally, your team will want to work and solve every challenge because they love the work they do and want to work hard for you because you care for them and they feel valued as a part of the team. Your clients will never stop coming because you operate with integrity and put their interest at the forefront as you make decisions in alignment with the purpose of the company. Everything in your business works as a beautiful symphony because you created it that way from the beginning.

CHAPTER 4

QUITTERS NEVER PROSPER: THE NO QUITTERS' MINDSET AND WHY NO QUITTERS WIN IN REAL ESTATE

L ife regularly presents opportunities for us to grow, both personally and in business. Building my business has brought
immense challenges, some of my own making and some
that simply appeared. Whether it was deciding what to do with
a property or who to hire or fire on our team, there have always
been dynamic and complicated problems. But my sincere realization going through every experience is there will always be
problems to solve and complex situations to overcome.

A personal mantra of mine for a long time now has been this: Ask for what you want, but be prepared to get what you asked for. If you want to change your life through real estate, you will have to solve problems and persevere through issues that seem impossible in the moment. Over and over, you'll have to decide whether the life you've imagined is worth being uncomfortable. To accomplish your goals, you'll need to operate on a regular basis in the uncomfortable zone between what you know and what you don't know yet. You must be willing to live and grow. Embrace your capacity to learn.

Post-bankruptcy was a challenging environment for me personally and professionally. I was still reeling from the pain of failing and the fear of what the future held. I struggled to understand what my next move should be and how I should navigate my new normal. One thing was clear—nothing was going to stop me from accomplishing my goals. I was going to get back into real estate. With lessons learned from the past, I was determined to create a better and more robust business. Not that I had any idea what that actually meant, but there was nothing to keep me from figuring it out. We get to decide what we want, how bad we want it, and what we are willing to do to accomplish it.

My goal of changing my life through owning real estate hadn't changed, but other things definitely had. I had almost no cash and a horrendously bad credit score that scared off all bank and hard money lenders, who were more focused on my assets, or lack of them, than on me. For months, I searched online for available real estate to purchase, and there were many potential opportunities to buy, but I couldn't do anything without a lender of some sort saying yes. Over six months I made twenty-plus requests for approval for funding for investment properties, and every single response I received was a no.

The Lunch That Changed My Life

During my time in Florida, several people spoke of a real estate investor, Rob, who had built an amazingly successful business. After my bankruptcy, I tried to find out as much as I could about him. Even though I did my research, I still didn't get exactly how Rob's business operated. I thought if I could understand his business, learn his secret, I would know how to build my own to be successful and thriving. I became fascinated and desperately wanted to set up a meeting with him.

I called and called, asking to take Rob to lunch, and he finally agreed. Little did I know that the lunch would be a life-changing window into a totally different and significant real estate business and also the beginning of a more than decade-long friendship.

On the day of our first meeting, Rob pulled into the huge parking lot of the large retail development filled with big-box stores and restaurants as I waited excitedly and impatiently for him to walk up. He stepped out of his nice but under-the-radar dark-green SUV and approached me in unassuming shorts and a dark polo shirt. He had the calm and powerful presence of a man who was crushing it in his life.

"Good afternoon, Rob, it's so great to meet you!" I said while throwing my hand out for a solid handshake.

"Nice to meet you as well, Nathan," he said in his deeply resonant voice.

We walked into the seafood restaurant and were greeted by a young and vivacious hostess who took us right to a good-sized booth toward the back of the dining area. I had so many questions I wanted to ask, but at the time, what I wanted to know most was how much real estate investors made, how many units they owned, and how in the world they were able to create a solid and prospering business for themselves.

"Rob, thank you again for taking the time to meet me for lunch," I told him. "It really means a lot." At that time in my life, I admit, I didn't fully appreciate the value of his time and knowledge. I continued, "I am dying to know what it is that you actually do." For several months, I had spent endless hours looking at his website, trying to grasp what his operation looked like. Rob looked at me, grabbed a small white drink napkin from the table, and began to draw a simple picture.

"Nathan," he said, "I like to think about my business like three-legged stool. Without all the legs, it would not be stable and would fall. My business has different supporting legs that all come together not only to make everything more stable but to help serve each other as well."

This is getting good! I thought to myself. "Makes sense," I said, "So you have different areas or divisions of your business, you are saying?"

"Exactly. Yes, we own rental properties, and we leverage and grow that portfolio for cash flow and building wealth over time. But we also own a property management company and a real estate brokerage. The property management company manages not only the properties we own, but as clients in the brokerage want to own rental properties, we are able to not only help them buy properties but manage them as well."

I said with excitement, "So you are able to not only buy and hold the properties for yourself, but in this case, you help your clients buy them and manage them too."

"Yes, from a cash-flow perspective, we are paid commissions from clients buying and selling real estate. Every month, the property management company charges our clients fees to manage their properties so that it has its own cash flow. And then with the rentals, we continue to buy and hold more and more houses. So they create cash flow, and every month, we make our mortgage payments on the ones we don't own outright, and the principal amount we owe on them goes down. And the best part is that the tenants are the ones paying that mortgage down."

Rob went on to explain that he would buy, renovate, and flip houses, almost always out of his IRA. Unreal. I had to step back to try to understand. "How do you even do that?" I asked. As he made more money from all of the operations of his business, he built and grew a lending company from his cash as well.

I was beginning to see how it all worked, and it was like seeing in color for the first time. Rob had laid out his multimillion dollar operation in just a few minutes on a napkin. For him our time together was just another meeting, not a big deal, but for me it provided a life-changing vision of what my business and my experience could be.

Sometimes there are moments that spark the lightning and blow the winds of change in our lives, and this lunch was just the storm and the inspiration I needed. It was an epiphany. Always be open, present, and willing to experience a moment, a lesson, or a relationship that will change your life forever. So, a year or so after that lunch, I called Rob, and once again I was asking for something from him to help me. How bad did I want it? Pretty bad!

"Hi, Rob, how are you, sir?" I asked. "Thanks for taking the time this morning. I know you are a busy man, so I'd love to get right to the reason I called if you don't mind."

"Great, Nathan, I appreciate that. What do you have going on?" he asked.

"As you know, I went through bankruptcy in the last year, and it has been really awful. I never thought I would end up having to deal with that in my life, but my wife and I have done our very best and are now in a position that we want to invest in real estate again."

"Okay, what did you have in mind?" he said with curiosity in his voice.

"I have a great deal that I want to purchase, but I am missing a key component. I've been able to save up some cash for repairs, but I need help with a lender on the purchase. It was my hope that you might be interested in lending on this deal for me?" I asked, so anxious that I could barely breathe as the words left my mouth.

"Tell you what," he said softly, "send over the details of the deal with the price, cost of repairs, value of the house, and the loan amount you are looking for, and I will take a look."

"Great!" I said. "I have everything together. I will fire it over to your email now." As promised, I sent everything over to him immediately, laying out my plan for the project clearly and concisely, stating how long it was projected to take and what I was asking from him. You probably recall a time when you wanted something to work so bad that your brain couldn't concentrate on anything else. I couldn't get anything done the rest of that day other than checking my text messages and emails hoping to read the three letters that I thought would change my life.

The day felt like weeks, but finally, I received a very short reply. "Looks good, Nathan, let's do it. I'll send you over the details, and we can get this funded for you."

Rob and I have continued to stay connected, but mostly via text and email, or an occasional phone call. To this day, having known him for well over ten years, I've only spent time with him in person two times. Both were early on after I first met him. But he has been and continues to be an absolutely invaluable and generous friend and mentor.

Remain Positive in All Things

When I first met Rob, I wasn't in a position to do anything to really help him, but I brought what I had to the table: positivity, gumption, and the desire to win. I told the truth about my mistakes and what went wrong, and he saw that I was willing to get back on the field to play the game even though the first pass didn't happen at all the way I had intended. We get to make a decision every day whether we are positive or not, so bring that intention to everything you do and every interaction you have.

Meeting and connecting with people is not hard to do, but it might seem like a daunting task from where you are. The problem isn't that the people you need or want to help aren't in your life or known by someone you are already close to. Most likely, they are already there. What matters is the approach and mental attitude you bring to interactions and conversations. Smiling and being kind when you meet people. Treating others with respect and bringing positivity to the relationship make people want to be around you, help you, and connect with you. Both positive and negative energy are magnets; whichever you put into the world, you will attract.

Being positive also helps when you don't feel like your goal will ever be reached. You have a decision to make: Am I mentally going to crack and get upset, or channel that energy I am feeling into taking action that gets me closer to my goal? Either way, you will expend effort that leads toward something.

Negativity takes so much mental space. It's heavy to carry in your body and your mind. Your heart is weighed down, and you have the feeling that whatever is wrong in your life will never change for the better. If you want to achieve something incredible in your life and do it with other amazing people, don't give negativity any place to live and grow. Your choice to create a life includes choosing how it feels to live it every single day. Do you want to choose feeling deeply happy and fulfilled, or feeling discouraged, frustrated, and sad? Your decision, your life, so choose wisely.

Even in moments that are difficult, we still have the power of choice. Something happens, no problem. Name whatever the issue is, and attack it. Solve the root problem and learn all the lessons. Don't dwell on screwing something up; focus on how to navigate the problem in the future. Cultivate gratitude and appreciation for the hard moments, and take it all in. Use these moments as the training ground for the positive, powerful, and incredible person you are becoming every day.

Don't Beat Yourself Up: You Just Haven't Learned the Lesson Yet

If you often say to yourself "I'm an idiot," or "I messed up again," that ends today. No more negative conversations with yourself. Those aren't serving you, and they certainly aren't helping you accomplish what you want to in your life. There is a big difference between a lesson that you need to learn, maybe more times than you would like, and not being smart enough to figure it out.

Lessons almost always come in the form of some sort of failure. So many times in business, I've found myself saying, "Wait, I'm here again? Facing the same problem that I screwed up before?" Maybe I hired yet another new employee and then neglected to give enough time and attention to onboarding and training them, and consequently, they weren't successful. Yes, I made this mistake over and over.

I didn't actually see the problem or my part in it until it was pointed out to me by someone on our team. This person not only could see the issue with our hiring process but also had a solution. She changed the process and created new and effective training programs. I couldn't pinpoint what in the hiring process was going wrong, so I wasn't effective in solving the problem.

I had to learn not to obsess over whether I was the person to solve the problem, and to not get frustrated and negative over failing to understand what to do (and then complaining and doing nothing). Ask for help and bring a positive attitude, a willingness to learn, and the grace to accept and celebrate someone else's perfect solution.

Imperfect Action Trumps Your Analysis Paralysis

No matter how pumped up you are about your favorite real estate podcast, book, or television show, or how much detail you have filled in on a spreadsheet, these are only tools. Tools won't take action for you. They don't pull the trigger on buying an investment. Of course, they are useful in providing inspiration or roadmaps for how you might get to your dream. But only you can take action and make things happen. My absolute favorite quote is from a 1910 speech by Theodore Roosevelt—popularly called "The Man in the Arena." In it, he describes how it feels to put yourself on the line in an attempt to accomplish something big. Here is an excerpt:

It is not the critic who counts; not the man who points out how the strong man stumbles, or where the doer of deeds could have done them better. The credit belongs to the man who is actually in the arena, whose face is marred by dust and sweat and blood; who strives valiantly; who errs, who comes short again and again, because there is no effort without error and shortcoming; but who does actually strive to do the deeds; who knows great enthusiasms, the great devotions; who spends himself in a worthy cause; who at the best knows in the end the triumph of high achievement, and who at the worst, if he fails, at least fails while daring greatly, so that his place shall never be with those cold and timid souls who neither know victory nor defeat.

You will not have the same information or the same level of understanding a year from buying your first investment as you do just talking or thinking about it today. No book is going to solve that nor will a podcast or a conversation with a friend or mentor. Actually pulling the trigger, living the experience, and taking the action will. It doesn't matter how much study and pondering you do. If you don't take action, it's like being a world-class athlete who only practices and never competes. It's time to put yourself in the game.

By having a clear vision of what you want, you make the strategy to get you there easier to identify, and the steps to take should be right in front of you. If you continue to find yourself having a hard time making a start, go back to the vision you laid out for your life. My guess is that it's either not clear enough to make you sure of the action to take or the vision isn't compelling enough to get you to move from where you are to where you think you want to be. Engage your positive mental attitude, go back and do the work of clarifying what you want your life to be about—how you want it to look and feel in your daily experience—and try again. This is not a failure on your part. It's a lesson in what you don't want, and it's incredibly important to learn and understand today so that you don't spend any more time working toward a goal that isn't compelling to you.

Root for Yourself—and Your Competition

Being happy in your own life is wonderful, but wanting everyone else to experience the same degree of happiness as you is absolutely freeing. It demonstrates an understanding there is enough in the world for each person to have what they want in life. Your dream should not be at the expense of others. You are not hoarding what you can while others have to give up what they want in life for you to have yours. This is not the way things actually work, and it's also a negative mindset to live with and put into the world.

Having an incredibly powerful purpose and vision for your life creates a stabilizing force that assures you of who you are today, where you are going, and what you are doing with your precious time on this planet. You can purposefully build whatever you want in life. Mentally, emotionally, and physically, you must become the person that you need to be to live the life that you want.

You can also harness and direct the positivity and energy of others to help them find and create that same purpose for themselves. Everyone needs to discover something they love to do, create, or learn about. How can you spark a life-changing moment for someone else? We won't be fully content ourselves without believing anyone, including our perceived competition, can also create what they want. Your success is not predicated on someone else failing.

Be an Obsessive Learner

Without moments in our lives that challenge our thinking or what we know to be true, like my meeting with Rob, we aren't growing and learning. Bringing a deep sense of purpose, the power of positivity, and an attitude and appreciation of learning to every interaction is something I constantly work on. Learning is a fun challenge, and when you've lined up what you want to do with who you are, you won't be able to stop the voracious desire to learn and grow. It will benefit every aspect of your life.

The answer to the problem you are struggling to solve right now is out there in front of you. It's also probably free of charge, in a book at the library or in a podcast episode on your phone. With information so freely available and so many teachers, mentors, and coaches who know what they are doing, you have no excuse. Seek them out, ask your deepest questions, and solve your biggest problems.

When I am working on a new problem that I have yet to understand the solution for, I have a method. I sit with the question or issue, which I have written out on paper or in a note on my phone, and then I do one of two things. I either listen to a podcast or call a friend. If the question or problem I am trying to solve is new, I like listening to a podcast where people talk openly about things they are working on. I am constantly inspired by stories and topics totally unrelated to my own life or business. They give me fresh perspectives and new insights. Podcast hosts like Tim Ferriss, Jocko Willink, and Joe Rogan have helped me learn and grow in ways I just wouldn't have been exposed to without listening to their shows.

My other strategy is to call a friend. Before I do that, I let the problem roll around in my brain for a bit. After a while, I come back to the original question and ask myself is it really that question? Have I gotten to the root? Or am I now seeing the issue from a different perspective, allowing me to hone the question, bringing it into sharper focus?

Once I have the problem nailed down, I'll think of who I know in my network of friends and mentors who would have the best understanding of my problem. I never assume anyone has time to spend with me, and I always start those conversations by clearly stating the problem I am trying to solve, how much time I am asking for, and that no is okay if they don't have time. I value them and their time and appreciate whatever will work for them. They have to win, too.

Always prepare for a call or in-person meeting. That means having a plan of what you specifically want to review and talk about. Send whoever you're meeting with an email with your questions in advance so they can be prepared to share the most pertinent advice. When you arrive or begin the call, start by thanking them for their time. Honor the time and space you have requested. Stay off your phone and email. Give them your full attention just as you would expect from them. As they share ideas, resist the urge to disagree or to explain why you don't think they will work. You asked for help, so be appreciative and pay close attention. Learn whatever you can. The ideas shared don't have to become your plan or even part of your plan, but you do owe the other person respectful listening.

These kinds of meetings have created such massive value for me in my life that I've started calling them Million Dollar Calls. Every week, my goal is to explore one opportunity, have one conversation, or start one new relationship that could lead to a million dollars. But, I don't go into the call telling the other person I'm looking for a million-dollar opportunity. Instead, I share with them how much I value them and that I want to spend time together to see how we could help each other. These calls lead to new learning and new opportunities all the time. Even just hearing how someone structured their deals or traveled the world and grew their business at the same time has opened possibilities for me and different ways of thinking. I know this: I've never left a call without a takeaway that was useful, impactful, or even business-changing.

Find the Best Mentors and Colleagues Who Want You to Crush Life

I would not be where I am in my business or enjoying the life I've created without the help of many mentors and friends. These people have given me countless hours of their time and exponentially increased my knowledge. I've listened to their struggles and their big wins and breakthroughs. We don't have to learn everything on our own. In fact, I'd say that we are so much better off not only learning from others but connecting with people who have similar goals. Whether a friend or a paid mentor, a like-minded person is someone who can see where you want to go. They might even help guide you back to your vision when you diverge from your path.

There are a few people I regularly spend time with in the real estate world. We share freely the kinds of deals, volume, and money we are making. We also share the challenges in our businesses and even what's happening at home. Being vulnerable and transparent helps us build more connection and better relationships. Our friends know who we are, have a deep understanding of our businesses and families, and connect our purpose to the actions and decisions we make.

Over the years, my business partner and I have had many paid coaches who helped us solve a multitude of challenges in the business. The coach or mentor you need right now is not likely the same one you'll need two, three, or five years from now. Find a coach who understands what you want to create in your life and can help you put the pieces in place. Go into new relationships with the belief they will work, but also discuss in advance what it would look like if it doesn't work and how you would dissolve that working relationship. Those conversations are so much easier ahead of time instead of after an issue or disconnect has happened.

Spending money on a coach when it feels like you don't have money to invest can seem counterintuitive, scary, or even dangerous, depending on your financial situation. Think of it this way: If you spent ten thousand dollars on coaching in the next year but made far fewer mistakes and were able to accomplish the goals you laid out with more clarity and confidence, would that investment be worth it? The answer has always been yes for me. Over and over, my investment in coaching and personal education has paid off. My partner and I now spend an average of well over six figures a year on coaching because it is that important to us personally and to our team.

You will need other people to help you accomplish what you want. Believing otherwise is a lie you are telling yourself—a broken mindset not grounded in reality. The areas where you feel resistance in your life are the very places you need to crack open to the daylight because you aren't willing to grow or learn in them. The belief that you are the only one who can solve your problems will forever diminish your ability to execute your plans and create the most amazing life you want. And if you are this far along in the book, you have clearly already committed to the idea that anything less than the life you want to live is unacceptable.

Automate and Delegate—and Bring Massive Value

The more time I spend doing things I want to, the more joy and happiness I have. My work and the business I own are tools to help me live the life I want and allow me to be around other people who want to create amazing lives for themselves. My work is not who I am, but just a component of my life.

As my business has expanded and we've gotten better at leading and growing our team, my personal responsibility and importance in the business have changed. I haven't looked at a specific house we were buying or selling in years. We have people on our team to do that. I no longer negotiate the funding of a deal or the date a house will be bought or sold. Nor do I get involved in the payments of rents or communications with the property management company managing our rentals. There are other people who love what they do who handle those responsibilities in the business.

When you create clarity about the business you want to have and the life you want to live, you are able to share those visions effectively. That focused communication makes it possible for others to join you, doing amazing work that you either aren't good at or no longer want to do. You can forever let go of the notion that you are the only one who can do that job or perform that task. That's a lie you are telling yourself, so stop telling it. You only achieve freedom to live your dream life when you finally give space for someone else to hold responsibility. You are designing your business to give you more time to do the work that you really love to do.

As you become more financially successful, you will have the incredible chance to help transform someone else's life. In our business, we tie a quarterly bonus for the entire team to the financial performance of the company. The better we do as a team at hitting our goals, the better everyone on the team does financially. When the team works well and compensation improves, there is a clear shift in positive thinking, problem-solving, and the outcomes of our projects. We want to reward for achieving those outcomes while also creating an environment of fun and success for everyone. Your team is your most important asset, so treat them with the love and care they deserve.

Moving out of day-to-day operations and turning over some of your roles leaves space to give back in ways you might not have considered. As your time commitment to work changes, you have more space in your day to help change the lives of those around you. You can focus on helping create a financial plan to put someone's kids through college or grow their own real estate portfolio. All of these touchpoints bring both positive change for them and a feeling of satisfaction for you. Great relationships are one of the biggest rewards in the pursuit and experience of living an extraordinary life.

CHAPTER 5

SOLUTION: REAL ESTATE DONE RIGHT

Doing something right doesn't mean that every action, every step, and every outcome will happen exactly as you expect or plan. Done right doesn't mean done perfectly either. Perfect doesn't exist, so let it die a fast death and let it go. What does exist is an outcome so clear, so compelling that you are willing to do whatever it takes to accomplish it. It's right there in your heart and mind as you let yourself believe just a little more deeply that something so life-changing can actually happen.

Real estate done right is setting whatever goal it is that you deeply desire and doing the work to achieve it. It is also the first morning you open your eyes, take a breath, and say, "This is my incredible life as I dreamt it to be and cultivated seed by seed to fruition."

The Saturday Call with Abby

As I began my Saturday morning, I looked at my phone and read an early morning text message from my dear friend and our company's COO. Abby rarely sends me messages, especially on a Saturday, so it caught my attention.

"Nathan, I am so sorry to bother you. After you and I had chatted about what to do with our real estate portfolio, I have been thinking a lot about what our options are. Would you mind letting me take you up on a conversation at some point? Sorry to bother you on the weekend."

Abby and her husband had been investing in their own personal real estate portfolio for years.

I immediately replied: "You aren't bothering me at all! I love being able to look at the amazing work you've done and see how best I can help. Actually, what are you up to right now? I can give you a call if you have time."

Abby messaged me back: "You don't have to do that! But right now would work for me if that's possible."

I let her know I'd call her as soon as I had my computer opened so I could be completely present with her. I also asked for her to send me the meticulous spreadsheet she created showing the growing portfolio of properties that she and her husband had so brilliantly been acquiring over the past few years.

I stood in front of my wooden standing desk in my beautiful basement home office and dialed her number.

"Abby! This is so fun! Thanks for sending me the message and trusting me to look at your properties with you."

"Of course," she said. "I know you help our clients all the time with this kind of thing, and I just don't know quite what to do. We've worked really hard and want to make sure we have the best possible plan in place."

I asked to look at the spreadsheet, and we engaged in some small talk about their finances. They had done an awesome job of saving and had substantial personal cash reserves and little debt. As I began to dig into the portfolio, I noticed that they had significant equity. Equity is the difference between what the property is worth and the amount they owe. All of a sudden, I got insanely excited.

"Abby, remind me again what you said you owed on your house." She told me and then asked me why.

"Well, I am not sure what you want to do with this portfolio, but I have a wild idea. I know you guys have the amount of cash that makes you comfortable, so you don't really need more, right?"

She agreed, clearly with a question in her voice as she wondered where I was going with this question.

"This might not be what you want at all, but I have an exciting idea. Today's interest rates are quite a bit lower than the rates you are currently paying on your investment properties, so refinancing those loans would automatically reduce your payments drastically. You could actually refinance the portfolio to 70 percent of the current value, and with the cash you could take tax-free from that refinance, you would be able to pay off the mortgage on your personal house!" I was fired up.

The line was quiet for a moment, and then almost in tears, Abby said, "Oh my gosh, you are totally right. And the values I have on the properties might even be pretty conservative compared to what they actually are."

We talked for a few more minutes about what lender to use and how to get the best result. I would always rather work with a lender who understands and does real estate investments than shop for the absolute lowest price and deal with someone who isn't familiar with real estate. I recommended she work with an awesome bank that could produce the exact result that she and her husband wanted. They had worked diligently for years to create a million-dollar portfolio and were now in a position to pay off their personal residence, but we had to make sure they ended up with the actual outcome they wanted. Paying off the mortgage on their personal house was a life-changing goal, and it was about to happen.

Less than a month later, I received a text message from Abby: "My husband is at the bank as we speak, sending the wire paying off our house!!! I can't believe it. Thank you again for helping us see what we could do. This is a moment we couldn't even see was possible. Thank you!"

Real estate done right will change your life forever.

Why I Love Real Estate

Real estate offers so many diverse ways to invest. There are endless opportunities and strategies you can employ. Not only can you buy real estate with the money you have earned, but you can add value to what you bought by updating it, or create more value by changing its type or class (such as residential to commercial). All these options allow you to find what kind of investing you like to do and create a business around what you want your life to look like.

Owning real estate doesn't mean you have to live in the same place where your investment property is located. Many clients we have worked with over the years have purchased in other markets because the prices of those properties were much less expensive than the market where they lived. They could create more cash flow, the amount that they received every month, using the difference between the rent the tenant paid and the mortgage they owed. You also don't need to know how to fix a broken toilet or rent out a property and manage the tenant to own and grow a real estate portfolio. I want you to envision what owning your business looks like, not try to learn and do every aspect of what needs to happen within it.

The Power of Leverage

Tell your stockbroker that you want to pay $40,000 for $200,000 of stocks. Good luck with that! Of course, there are other vehicles like stock options, but you aren't buying the stocks, you only have an option to buy them at a certain price for a dollar amount. In real estate, you can take that same $40,000 and use it as a 20 percent down payment and let the bank loan you the other 80 percent. This example is called a conventional loan. There are other loan types such as VA, USDA, and FHA loans that require little to nothing down depending on your circumstances. With real estate you have a supersized chessboard and almost infinite strategies and plays you can make to fit what you want to accomplish.

Using loans, or leverage as we call it, also allows you to own and control way more real estate than you would have been able to buy with the cash you have in hand. If you have $100K to invest with 80 percent bank financing, you could buy around $500K worth of real estate. With $200K, you can own your first million in real estate. Abby did it, I've done it, and so can you.

The other amazing part of using leverage is that as the rent is paid, cash flow is earned, so you are always paying down the principal on the balance of the loan. Every month, the balance owed goes down and the equity in your investment property goes up. Someone else is literally making you wealthier every time they pay their rent, and you in turn pay your mortgage.

Everyone Needs a Place to Live

The most basic human needs are water, food, and shelter. We are in the shelter business. Owning real estate is not taking advantage of people, stealing their money, or denying them an opportunity to own their own home. People choose to live in a rental home for various reasons: not wanting to deal with maintenance, recent changes in their life like graduating from school or a marriage, or moving and changing jobs. You have the opportunity to provide an amazing place for someone to live and create a home for themselves and their family.

Every property we own we renovate or build to a predetermined high standard of quality. You always want to decide the types and locations of properties you acquire and the standard at which you maintain them. It's critically important to me the properties we own are well renovated and regularly maintained. Not only is this the best policy for the health of your property, but it's also in the best interest of your tenant. In the end, the value of the house depends on how well it's maintained and the relationship with the tenant, who you want happily living in the house for years to come.

Real Estate Is Awesome

There is no hiding my insatiable passion. I love real estate—creating amazing opportunities for our business to invest in various projects and properties. Think of the tremendous impact you would make buying and renovating dilapidated houses and transforming them to beautiful homes. Awesome, right? It's exciting to create opportunities that are wins for our team, our clients, and communities.

I've always loved to think outside of what "normal" might be, and that is what real estate has allowed me to do every day. I look at a property and dissect what the best use of it might be. Do I rent it out, or sell it to a buyer as their own home, or turn it into a chic vacation rental home for thousands of guests to enjoy over the coming years. I live to create interesting deals through thoughtful negotiation or creative structures, and I want you to find that same passion for whatever real estate business you want to create.

Don't have enough money to put down on purchasing that first house? No problem. Ask the owner of the property to help you with the down payment or bring in a partner to supply the cash while you put the deal together. Or find a great group of homes you want to hold as rentals, bring in a few friends, and pool your money together to create a new home-buying group that takes down bigger portfolios of homes or apartments. You will never again say to yourself, "I can't invest in real estate because . . ." Instead, you will say, "That looks like an awesome opportunity. *How* can I put that together?"

Have you dreamt forever about owning a beach or lake home? No problem. You can even turn your dream vacation home into an asset that pays you to own it. Find the perfect property, buy it with your cash or a creative deal structure, and set up the property as a vacation rental. A vacation rental can create even more cash flow than a regular long-term rental with a tenant, but make sure you review the comps for rentals in the area, and plan on a higher vacancy rate. In the first years, rent out the property more than you use it, and take the additional income to pay it down. Eventually, you can pay it off using the money that other people pay you to stay there while vacationing. You'll have your beach house and have it paid off over time.

Tried-and-True Method of Building Wealth

Investing in real estate is not a "get rich" scheme. It is, however, a long-term plan to make you wealthy. The wealthiest people in the world have used real estate to grow their net worths and pay less in taxes. You can also pass your wealth on to your heirs through trusts and other real estate strategies that helps preserve your assets for generations to come.

As your real estate portfolio grows, so will your net worth and the cash flow you receive every month—and your ability to buy more property increases. The more cash flow you receive every month and the more you net from it, the more you have to reinvest in real estate. Over time, these incredible real estate investments will compound and grow exponentially even if you stop investing cash or buying more properties.

Just as you can grow and compound individual properties in your portfolio, you can choose different asset classes to invest in. There are single-family homes, self-storage units, apartments, and even syndications in which other investors put together deals that you invest your cash in. The type of investment you make must directly link back to the big vision you have, the amount of money you want to actively earn, and the wealth you want to produce from all the effort. Every decision, every investment, must always link back to the big vision of the life you want to live and the impact it will have.

Understanding the Superpower That Is Real Estate

Leverage is an incredible tool that allows you to grow and scale your real estate portfolio at a dramatically faster scale. Banks and other lending institutions will allow you to purchase a property after establishing what it is worth through an appraisal and how much they want to lend. You provide only a portion of the value in cash to buy the property. Once the property is purchased, many other amazing factors will come into play over time.

One factor is that as you pay the mortgage each month, the principal balance, or the money that you owe the lender, decreases. The lower the interest rate you have on the mortgage, the less money you pay in interest, and the more that goes to principal. The longer the period of the loan, typically thirty years, the lower the payment but the less that goes to principal. With a fifteen- or twenty-year mortgage, the payment is higher, but the amount of money going to principal is also higher, and paying off the mortgage over time is faster.

Over a few years, the mortgage will continue to get paid down, which creates even more options. The property could have gone up in value, stayed the same, or in some circumstances, even gone down in a down market. Don't panic. This is a long game, and we are playing to build massive wealth, not get in and out of properties and lose sight of the incredible life that we are building.

I have almost always made money in the form of higher property values when I've invested over a longer period of time; I'm thinking three to five years. To be very clear, I don't assume values always go up—but it's a great bonus. As the mortgage is paid down, the value increases, and the difference between what you owe on the property and its value grows. That amount is called the equity in your property. For instance, if you buy a house for $200K and put $40K down, you would owe $160K. Let's say you do a thirty-year mortgage and have an interest rate of 3 percent based on the current market. In three years, you should see a modest increase in the value by an additional 3 percent per year. The value of the house is now $218K. You've also paid down a little more than $10K on the mortgage. So, the total amount of equity in your house is now $218K (value) - $150K (mortgage) = $68K!

I love real estate!

One word of warning on using appreciation in your calculation. **I don't ever assume that any amount of appreciation will happen when I make my decision on purchasing a property.** This is only a bonus, though it's something that has occurred often in my experience. Don't get crazy or complacent when you decide to pull the trigger and purchase an investment. Be conservative, and make the best possible decisions you can based on the information you have today like the value of the property, what it will fetch in rent, and the taxes and insurance you will have to pay on it. Make sure it's a solid purchase that fits the criteria of what you are buying now.

If you want to add properties to your portfolio, any real estate you already own could be used as a tool for purchasing more. Using the same example of the $200K property, the $68K in equity gives you more interesting options. There are a few different ways you could approach the next steps you take, depending on your overall strategy.

You could decide to put a line of credit on the property, which allows you access to a portion of the equity. Then you could use that money to invest in other properties. Just remember you still have to make payments on the loan you've taken until it is paid back on your line of credit, so account for that in your cash flow and property expenses. I love to look at the cash flow I am making on a new property or combined properties I now own, pay down that line of credit from the cash flow, and then repeat. You could also use the net cash flow you are making from additional rental properties to make payments on the line of credit so it's paid down even faster, and then repeat.

A refinance is another powerful option if you want additional cash to invest. Using the same example, let's calculate 80 percent of the new value: $218K ´ 80% = $174,400. There is a difference of roughly $25K between what you owe ($150,000) and the 80 percent of value the bank will lend you. After a new appraisal and paying the bank fees to close your loan, you will likely walk away with $20K or so, depending on what the actual costs are. Get this: The money you receive in a refinance is also *tax-free*, so you don't have to treat it like income. Make sure you review what the new cash flows are on the property you refinanced so that you understand the big-picture financial impact of your decision. Do you see how this is easily scaled?

Real estate just takes time, patience, and making the decision to take action.

If you don't want to take on additional debt, you could also decide to pay the mortgage down faster instead of taking out equity. In this way, you are reducing your debt and increasing the speed at which you pay the mortgage down. A really simple way to pay off your property faster is by doubling the amount of money that goes to principal every month. Google "mortgage calculator," and look at what's called the amortization schedule of your loan. This shows what portion of your payment goes toward the principal and how much of it goes to the bank for the use of their money. If you double the amount going to principal, which is much less than the amount going toward interest, you can effectively pay the property off twice as fast. With a standard thirty-year mortgage, if you double your principal, you can have the entire house paid off in roughly fifteen years.

Some investor friends of mine use this style of investing to dramatically grow their net worth. They don't need or want the short-term cash flow from their rental properties, so they use it to pay down the principal. Imagine that you bought five properties that averaged $200K in value, the figure we used in the example. Even with *zero* appreciation, if over the next fifteen years you double the amount you paid to principal, you would have a net worth of *one million* dollars, plus the cash flow from five free and clear properties you own. Do you think having the patience to invest over the next fifteen years of your life is worth being a millionaire? *I think so.* You can do it, too. You just need to make the decision and take the action to create the incredible life you have wanted.

Now let's take this journey to completion. Let's say you start investing at age twenty-five. It takes you five years, one house per year, to acquire the five properties, but you've also begun to pay off the principal of the first property, just as I explained. At age thirty, then, you own five properties, and the first property you purchased is now just ten years from being paid off. When you turn forty, the first property you purchased is now completely free and clear, and you can compound paying off the other four even faster by using all of the cash flow now coming from that property. At age forty-five, you have a *million*-dollar portfolio with no debt and awesome cash flow coming in every month.

Depending on your goals, you now have even more interesting options because you have put in the work and created the opportunity for yourself. You could sell those properties and do a 1031 exchange in which you take the properties you own, defer taxes, and buy something much bigger like an apartment building or a group of homes. You could continue to own those properties but decide to put a line of credit on them. Utilize a portion of that equity to buy another group of properties, either with cash from that equity or by leveraging another five properties and repeating the process.

In building your portfolio you have as many options as you have ideas. You can decide for yourself how many properties you want to buy, over what period, and if you want to continue to grow with higher leverage or pay them down as fast as possible. All of these decisions should align directly with the income you want to create and the lifestyle you want to live.

The important thing to remember is that there is not a wrong answer whatever you decide. Make your choices based on what you want to create, knowing as you begin that whatever you decide will take time but will be worth the investment in cultivating the life you want. Real estate is an incredible tool and one that has fundamentally changed my life. You can decide right now that you want to scale and grow your portfolio, but in a few years, you can decide that you own enough properties to pay them down and lower the leverage in your portfolio. The choice is yours. Allow yourself to imagine taking the action, being successful, making these decisions, learning the lessons, and crushing your real estate business. That experience and the life you want is right here.

CHAPTER 6

THE VISION: HOW REAL ESTATE INVESTING HELPS YOU BUILD AN EXTRAORDINARY LIFE

I have the deepest appreciation for the time and financial freedom my real estate business has given me. I've come to realize that I cherish the little things I've gained the most, like my ability to spend an hour on a weekday afternoon hitting golf balls, or taking my kids to the park, or enjoying a lively lunch with a friend complete with bourbon and cigars. My wife and I no longer make family choices based on what we can afford or when we can take time off; we base them on what we want to do and when we want to do it.

When I spend time with other people, it is with people I deeply appreciate and enjoy. We talk and learn together about business, philosophy, real estate, martial arts, and music. I have an incredible martial arts gym near my house where I love to train and a music room at home filled with guitars I love to play. I have created a weekly schedule that includes not just martial arts and music, but also meditation and journal time. Living the life I want means that I also regularly reflect on the choices and decisions I have made and whether they are still creating the life and happiness I want.

Your Incredible Life Is Right Here

One of the hardest lessons to learn is that the life you've been able to imagine or create up to now is the one that you are currently living. You have created your experience—your life—and you are responsible for where you are now. But you are also responsible for whatever comes next. You are at the helm of your future life.

I love football and am constantly impressed by the talent and skills of the guys who play the game. It goes without saying that the professional players at the highest levels have to put in an insane amount of work and time to be the best. But the nature of the game, what players must do on the field, requires a certain size, speed, and athleticism, which excludes most people from the profession, alas myself included.

You don't need to be built of solid muscle, run a lightning-fast forty-yard dash, or be able to catch a football while launching yourself headfirst in order to build a real estate business. It does not require exceptional genetics, abilities, or skills. Countless real estate investors have come before you and cleared the path, each making their own mark on what they wanted their businesses to look like. You only have to commit to putting in the work and making the constant effort to transform your life into what it can be.

It's okay if you aren't sure exactly what you want your future life to be. It can be hard right now to form a complete picture of what both your business and personal life will look like. But in this chapter, you are going to start laying everything out that you can see, and writing down areas that you aren't sure about yet so you can come back to them. As you keep revisiting those unclear details, you will find they start to fill in and your dream will continue to take shape. Give yourself permission to bring it to fruition.

Your Business Is Created to Serve You

It might seem selfish to think of your future business this way, but it's critical. Understand that your business is created to serve you and the life you want to live. Too often, young entrepreneurs get excited and set their sights on creating a business because they either have an idea or are tired of dealing with their boss. They start an enterprise without really knowing what its purpose is or how it will operate. If you don't have clarity about those details from the start, your business can quickly devolve into an unfulfilling job you hate and can't quit.

Even in my own business, I've had many seasons when I have worked harder and made less money than I could have working for someone else. That's why starting with the end result of what your business looks and feels like is so important. If you paint that future vividly enough, when you find yourself being challenged and facing adversity that you need to overcome, you will know exactly what goal you are working toward and why it is imperative you continue down the path. Make the business you build congruent with the life you want to live.

Give every layer of your business, the work you do, the life you want to have, and what you do with your time your full focus. Be obsessed with drilling down to uncover exactly what you want. Write out the challenges in your journal, forming them as questions, and work on them daily. *How do I want my business to be built? What does my typical day look like? Where do I live, and is the lifestyle this area offers congruent with what I want?* Spend time with the answers you begin to form to make sure they will be best for you long term. Don't just ask the difficult questions, but take time to also reflect on smaller issues that come up every day. Dig into them. Solve them. And integrate those decisions into your plan.

What Is the Perfect Business for You?

Your business must be built around the life and lifestyle you want to have. If you want to work five or ten hours a week, you will need a team who can operate the business without you. That team will require clear direction about what you want to happen. You'll need to have and communicate defined objectives and create a thriving leadership environment for whoever is running the operation. Want to make a million a year? Awesome, but what are you going to produce in your business that will consistently create that level of revenue so that you can receive that level of income? How many units will you need located in what part of the town or city to generate that cash flow? You will need a clear plan to create the life you want.

Maybe financial outcomes are less important to you than free time and a flexible schedule. Want to travel the world, regardless of your total income? Create a business with a few key team members, and keep your business and overhead small to allow for a perfect balance of profitability and simplicity. If you want to positively impact the lives of your team, you could give them bonuses based on their production so that when the company does better, you do better, and so do they.

A Purpose beyond Money

Dramatically increasing income is almost always what new real estate investors tell me is their primary focus. And it's one of the easiest things to accomplish and a leverage point that will help you if you use the money effectively. Personally, I also enjoy the chase of putting together deals and the insane fun it is to watch deals turn into dollars in real time. Making money is awesome, and I would not be able to live the lifestyle that I want without it. But it is only one of many tools that you can use to create your new experience of life.

I've found that as I've made more money and owned more real estate, I've also gained more time. I'm able to relax and be more present in whatever situation I'm in. I plan and take more family and personal time to do things I really enjoy. I've also found that I make difficult and complex business decisions more easily, because I can focus on the best long-term outcome—like being truly present in my day—instead of the next dollar and how it will affect my financial situation at the moment. Allow money to be a vehicle for living not the end goal.

Another objective you might consider that doesn't directly involve money is to create an inspiring work culture. You can develop a team that grows to become outstanding at their work and in creating the lives they want too. I've felt immense joy watching other people on our team succeed. I have seen them expand into their positions, taking what they have learned and making the business even better. It's an amazing experience to mentor someone, and then witness that person flourish, loving what they do and helping your business at the same time.

Creating an extraordinary life for yourself is a powerful goal, but holding that vision for the team around you is even more profound. You will realize that the business you are endeavoring to create is an extension of not just the life you want to live but encompasses others as they create, and build what they want their lives to be. The clearer your vision is, the more easily others around you will be able to see the life they want to live too. You have set the trajectory for yourself and expressed it in a way they are able to understand and use to visualize their own. In essence, by living your most extraordinary life, you are setting the stage for the people you care about and are closest to, to do the same.

How to Create Your Perfect Vision for Life

If you were handed a magic wand that allowed you to spend every day doing whatever you wanted, what would your life look like? Sure, making money might be a part of your vision, but remember, money is just a tool. How do you want to feel every day? And what would you do to produce that feeling over and over?

Here's a bit of my vision. For our family, we wanted to experience life being financially strong, taking time for regular travel, and adhering to a healthy lifestyle of great food and regular exercise. At work, I wanted to grow an awesome business, inspire our team, and find ways to help them to grow in their financial understanding. I wanted to build a culture and a mission that would fire them up. Another goal was to set my work team up to be financially secure long term with a generous income and substantial wealth by the time they retired. Personally, I wanted to do things regularly in life that would challenge me—that would inspire me to be a better man, a better dad, and a better husband. I wanted to find new ways to experience life by picking up new hobbies, like training for an MMA fight at nearly forty years old, going on difficult mountain hikes, and taking golf lessons with the goal to play a round under 100 in my first year of playing. I love being in the fire, personally challenged and having to work through it.

Write down specifics of what your life would look like. Name the emotions you want to feel, like joy, happiness, passion, love, excitement, fun, creativity, confidence, curiosity, or satisfaction. There are no wrong answers, but clarify the feelings you want to experience regularly and also those you don't want. Then, ask what you want to have or experience over and over? This is personal to you.

Often I've found that it's easier for people to describe the life they don't want to live than the life they do want. In order to define and create the life you want, you have to believe you can actually achieve it. Give yourself the grace to dream and believe it's possible. Remember to write down and visualize what it would look like. Then, talk about it with your family. Read what you have written every day, and decide whether you feel it is congruent with what you truly want. Share it with your closest friends. Believe deep down that whatever life you do want, it is possible to create.

Once you've defined the big picture, you can narrow your focus to what needs to be accomplished in the next few months. For years now, I have used this simple method to stay successfully connected to what I want my life to look like. Start by writing down three headings: "personal," "family," and "business." Now decide what you need to work on in each area. Journal about your experience and progress toward each goal for the next three months. Your focus should yield results you never experienced before.

Sometimes I need to work on a large-scale project, and sometimes it's a very small and detailed single issue. Your focus can even be a mental practice. Recently, I've had a personal goal to be more dialed in with my martial arts practice. So, I've been spending time journaling daily on what it is that I am working on in class, different aspects of my practice, and how they all connect. I've also wanted to increase my gratitude and positivity, so I focus daily on meditation, positive affirmations, and how to be more thoughtful with the people around me. Where you encounter regular mental resistance or challenges is where you should target your focus. This can be uncomfortable at first, but progress in these tougher areas yield the biggest dividends.

Without daily targeted focus on a goal listed under each of your headings, it is easy to slack off or totally miss a whole dimension of your life. For instance, when work was extremely busy and I was working a lot of hours, I had a tendency to miss opportunities with my family—like being present at home, regularly enjoying time playing with the kids, and going on fun weekly date nights with my wife. I also sometimes felt mentally or physically exhausted and decided to bail on regular exercise, journaling, or meditation even though I knew I would feel better if I did those things. That's why I write down something under each journal heading and keep focused on it. I also ask a few close friends to help me be accountable to whatever I've committed to do. Without routine purposeful focus on your business, personal, and family life goals, you will not experience the life that you want to create.

Simple and Clear Strategy

There are so many ways you can approach building a business around real estate. Often I find choosing one is the biggest challenge for new investors. Without a focus on one specific and measurable goal, it's easy to lose momentum and end up chasing random and incongruent opportunities.

Start with what you are most excited about in real estate, and grow that business until it can run without you. For me, by far the most exciting aspect of this journey is building an incredible real estate portfolio. In the short term, it takes time to build cash flow by adding more units. As time and the units you own grow, so does the wealth you are creating.

Focusing on one area helps you scale the business while also bringing in other people to help you run, manage, and handle the day-to day operations. If the focus is clear, you can name what the goals are, train people to help you do exactly what it is that you want to accomplish, and empower others to begin performing the work (which you would have had to do instead). That is what creating a business that serves your extraordinary life requires.

Master one strategy, and empower your team to run with that part of the business, and then you can begin to look at adding other verticals, or supporting legs, to the business. Those opportunities could be buying and renovating distressed properties, building new construction from the ground up, or scaling your portfolio with large apartment complexes. Dream about what kinds of opportunities you want to focus on next, but also refer back to the feelings and experiences you want to have in your life and use them as a litmus test. Will a new opportunity produce the positive and impactful experience and feeling that you want? If your answer is a resounding yes, move forward. If not, even if the opportunity would mean more money, it would detract from your goal of living your best, most amazing life. So, if the answer is not a resounding yes, you should definitely pass on pursuing the new venture.

As you make more money, you can also choose to invest in more passive opportunities like apartment syndications or lending your money to other people for their own investments. You must still do your homework, understand the business, and create a strategy around whatever it is that you decide to invest in. The friends and investors I look up to most, often have several kinds of investments, some meant to passively build long-term wealth and others to more actively create short-term income.

Create Flexibility and Space in Your Life

Creating the most extraordinary life means that every day, you are spending the majority of your time doing not just what you want to do but what is exciting and fulfilling. Take out a calendar, or even a piece of paper, and lay out a week on it. Start by filling in what you want to spend your time doing outside of work. Don't be shy or afraid that something is too expensive or unimportant. You are in the planning phase, and everything you do needs to be geared toward seeing, building, and then living the life you wish to create for yourself.

Be sure to go back to the three areas of your life—personal, family, and business—and ensure that all three areas are represented during the week you have plotted. You might want to start your day with meditation, reading, journaling, and prayer. You might want to add more exciting activities to your week—learning or being challenged in amazing hobbies that you love, for example. Or having dates with your spouse, maybe once a week for lunch and once a week for a lengthy date night with time for cocktails, dinner, and even music or a comedy club afterward. If you have children, take the time to plan not just time with them but amazing experiences that you can share with them and as a family. Beyond the weekly calendar, write down how often you want to travel and where. What are the inspiring destinations you want to visit, and what kinds of experiences do you want to have when you go? Fill out a daily, weekly, and monthly calendar that lets you wake up every day wondering how your life was so perfectly planned and executed. It will be hard to believe this could be your daily experience. It can.

No longer will your life revolve around what you can afford or not afford, but instead around what you want to do and how you want to live. This might feel difficult to envision at first, and that is totally normal. Allow yourself to sit in a feeling of joy. Imagine doing something you love, maybe walking on a beautiful beach. Dig your toes in the sand and feel the breeze. Once you are in that blissful state, you can more easily approach more ways you want to spend your time. Don't feel guilty about what you want. Put your energy into the vision you are creating, and see it as clearly and with as much color as you can.

Not only will you have complete latitude in creating the life you want, but the same goes for the business you create that gives you the time and financial resources to live the life you've planned out. You can choose the types of properties you want to invest in and where they are located, close by or hundreds or thousands of miles from where you live. What kind of design will you use in the interiors of the properties? Will you manage your own properties or hire an outside property management company? Would you rather have a large and robust organization, or do you want to keep it small and nimble? You get to decide exactly what the business does, how it operates, and how it serves you.

A Badge Protecting More Than a City

I remember Brian's New York accent as we began our call with a little small talk. He had come to us as a referral from another East Coast client. His daily experience was putting on a gun, a badge, and a police officer's uniform, and defending and caring for the public. Over the years, we have worked with lots of law enforcement, firefighter, and military clients, who made good money but wanted to grow and scale their real estate portfolios. I am to this day still deeply passionate about helping others learn and invest in real estate so I love every conversation. This one, with Brian, however, was about to take a completely unexpected turn. I had to solve a problem I had not encountered before.

Client conversations usually are about buying ten or twenty houses or creating five or ten thousand dollars in passive income per month. There are fairly common reasons for wanting to do this too. Maybe a client wanted to enable a spouse who didn't love their job to come home and be a full-time mom or dad.

Or maybe they wanted to pursue a personal business passion without the fear of not having that monthly W-2 income. This police officer who put his life on the line every day for his city, though, was putting his financial resources on the line to help someone else.

As the call unfolded, Brian explained to me that his son had special needs. He had to ensure that there was enough money to support his son even after he was no longer on the planet to do it. For the first time in my life, I truly saw how we were not just helping to create wealth for people; we were changing the way they could care for the people they love.

Real estate is a very powerful tool and financial vehicle that can be used for any purpose you want. Yes, you can create incredible wealth and income for yourself, but you can also change the life of someone else. You can help people you don't know by giving to amazing causes or you can care for someone close to you, like Brian did, by ensuring they can live out their remaining days in a way that you would want—even when you aren't physically there to support them. Sometimes the deepest and most fulfilling part of living an extraordinary life is being able to love and care for others.

You Are in Control of Your Outcome

I'm not a betting man, but I bet you don't have influence or control over the decisions that CEOs and corporate boards make when you invest in a stock. You are at the mercy of their vision and whatever factors they choose to consider in making decisions. The money you invest is simply added to the millions or billions of dollars that company is using in their massive operation. You can only hope that after some period of time, you will receive a return commensurate with the perceived risk of that investment. Investing in stocks does work, and there are people who make a great living or even retire on the value of their stock portfolios over time. But you have zero control over the outcome, and in the end, it is not your business. It is controlled by the companies you have invested in.

While building and growing your real estate business, you get to decide everything. Do you own large apartment complexes near airports in the largest cities, single-family homes in suburban neighborhoods, or even chic boutique hotels? Your call. Whatever it is that you are excited about or find interesting to learn about is where you should put your focus and invest. There isn't a board waiting to approve your business decisions or others trying to influence your investment, design, and strategy choices. Whatever the outcome of your investment decisions, they are one hundred percent yours to determine and execute.

Anyone Can Do It

Starting out, you don't have to quit your job and build a massive team to be successful in real estate. You might love your job and have no intention of quitting. You may simply want to control the direction of your investments and can see, as I did, that real estate is by far the best tool to help you achieve what you want. Over time, you might want to go out on your own and deal in real estate exclusively, but you don't have to. You can grow your business slowly, investing in real estate while working in the job or profession that you feel called to. Living your most extraordinary life involves setting yourself up to make the calls from now on, growing at the rate that you want to grow, and knowing that anyone can decide to invest in real estate as a life-changing move.

You may be entering real estate as a contractor, an engineer, or a real estate agent. Coming to investing from one of these professions is an advantage. You already possess some understanding of and access to the real estate world, even if you have not yet taken the plunge into owning or investing in your own portfolio. One choice for someone coming from one of these professions is to buy one, two, or maybe even three or four properties a year while continuing to grow and learn in the real-estate-related profession you are already in and enjoy. But tell everyone you work with that you are also now buying and investing in real estate. That way, as investment opportunities arise, more people are aware of what you are looking for and can help you build and grow your real estate business.

I'm not always the most patient person, and you might not be either. For me, I had to go all in and start building my new business like a maniac once I saw what real estate could create. In just our first year after starting Bridge Turnkey Investments, my business partner and I purchased over a dozen properties, and then we added thirty or forty in our second year. If that is you too, then go all in and get after it. Just be sure that you start with the foundation that we talked about in previous chapters. Lay out the vision, what it is that you want your life to look like, the types of investments you are going to focus on, and pick a direction. That way you won't look up a few months or years later and realize you have been all over the place in your decisions and failed to create the business or the life you wanted.

House hacking is also an excellent way to get started in investing, even if you keep your full-time job. Basically, you invest in the house that you live in. You may live there alone or with your family or you may even rent out open bedrooms to some housemates. Once the project is renovated and completed, you can either sell the house for a profit and put those funds back into a new house, or you can refinance it, keeping the house to either live in or rent out. Investing in real estate for you might be as simple as being able to buy and live in the house you've always dreamt of.

A dear friend of mine lives in California, where buying real estate is extremely expensive. He and his spouse used the house hacking strategy to buy and update multiple properties in succession, moving his family every few years into a new fixer-upper home. Within the last year or so, they were able to purchase a million-dollar home in an amazing location, with a pool in the backyard. They had taken their time, investing in properties they would live in while updating them. They were able to take the profits they made from each of the houses and roll them into the next house—one after another until they could eventually buy their dream house.

Regardless of whether you want to build a massive portfolio of rental properties, design and renovate, or just afford and scale to your dream house, you can do it. By visualizing the outcome, you will be able to see where you are going and take the calculated actions required to get you from where you are today to where you want to be. There is no special predisposition or innate gift that makes you a real estate investor from birth. You simply need to decide what it is you want your life to look like and take action every day. One house or one deal turns into two, and then into months of effort and learning. And then into another five or ten properties, or simply the house that will help you make a chunk of money so that you can buy and invest in the new property you want to own. Investing is not a race to own all the real estate you can. It is a deliberate strategy executed with patience and founded on an understanding of where you want to go. Stick with that course of action until you have accomplished your goal.

CHAPTER 7

TYPES OF REAL ESTATE BUSINESSES AND PROPERTIES: REAL ESTATE 101

I t's time to check in on how you are feeling about using real estate to change your life. Often the feeling I hear new students or investors in the real estate space express most strongly is fear. The fear of not knowing what precise steps to take or the fear of all the knowledge they will need to build the entire future business they want. This is normal. It's your mind's warning system letting you know you are entering something new and different. Fear does not signal that you can't accomplish what you want. It's telling you to pay close attention.

You've just embarked on something you haven't done before, eyeing whatever new real estate venture that fits your circumstances. With more time, knowledge, and investing experience, that fear will disappear. Just like riding a bike, playing a musical instrument, or engaging in almost any activity, skills, proficiency, and even elegance come with time and experience. But, you can't buy time and experience; you must do the work in front of you to accomplish what you want. And you are fully capable of learning all you need to learn, taking all the actions you must take, and creating the life you want to live.

Key Facets of Real Estate

Owning real estate is fantastic for building your net worth to a high level or for creating cash flow. There are five key components that make it so incredible: appreciation, depreciation, cash flow, leverage, and principal pay-down. Sometimes they work in conjunction, and sometimes investors decide that one or more elements of investing are more important to them than others. Again, there is no wrong answer. You simply need to have the foundational knowledge and understanding so that you can use and combine the components to create what it is you want.

We are going to spend some time in this chapter examining each of the five basic facets so you can begin that crucial learning. Without that understanding, you won't have the entire real estate investing picture or all the tools for fully analyzing investment opportunities.

Appreciation

Appreciation is the increase in the value of a property. There are two ways you can experience appreciation. One way is to buy a property that needs work at a cost that is under the value of that property after renovation. For example, let's say you purchased a house for $110K, and after walking the property with your contractor, you get a bid to totally renovate it and bring it back to life for $45K. Then you ask your realtor what the properties in the area that are comparable to yours when renovated will sell for. She tells you could expect to get $210K if you were to sell the house.

$210K completed value - ($110K purchase + $45K renovation) = $55K in equity.

In this example, you have created $55K in "forced" appreciation. By buying a property that needed work, spending the time and resources to bring the house back to a beautifully renovated state, you forced, or created, the appreciation in the value. You knew that increase was going to be the difference between the cost of purchasing the house plus the spend on construction and the amount it would be worth once completed.

Using forced appreciation works for those who want to adopt the BRRRR strategy and for those who want to fix and flip a house for cash. BRRRR stands for Buy, Renovate, Rent, Refinance, and Repeat. The end result is you renovated the property, put a tenant in it, and added it to your rental portfolio. In the fix-and-flip scenario, you would purchase the property, renovate with the intention of increasing the value of that property, and then sell it, earning the difference between what you put into the property and what it sold for.

Appreciation that is not forced, or created through upgrades to the house, happens over time as the market goes up in value.

As houses around yours sell for more than what you paid, your property value goes up too. I love appreciation and have benefited from it many times in our own investments. However, **we never assume a rate of appreciation beyond what we believe the value will be once our renovations are done**. Additional appreciation is a beautiful benefit, but don't let it cloud your decision making. Don't buy a property today that isn't a good deal because you think its future value could rise. Only underwrite your investments and make go/no-go decisions based on numbers you can see and understand—not what may happen in the market.

Depreciation

When you own real estate as an investment, you are able to take the total value of that property and depreciate it over time. In our business, every year our accountant calculates the amount of real estate we need to buy and hold to offset our projected income and tax burden for that year. The IRS allows real estate investors to depreciate real estate assets, which reduces the taxes you owe. Our intention is to buy enough real estate to pay as little tax as legally possible. Depreciation is a really powerful tool for people who want to grow and scale a large real estate portfolio because they will have a large deduction to write off against any active income they are making.

Depreciation is not a direct income source, but it is very much like a secondary income, especially if you are expecting to make other significant income. This works because you are able to write off a portion of the value of that property every year. As the home ages, things naturally will need to be fixed or replaced, and that is what the IRS is allowing for. In our business, we've paced the amount of real estate we buy and hold with the active income from our fix-and-flip business to keep our taxes as low as possible while still operating and making decisions that are legal and ethical.

Owning real estate brings all kinds of advantages, and we want to use all of the tools for our benefit, and not just ones that create income. Using the proven strategy of depreciation can help us retain the income we've worked so hard to create. The IRS allows you to depreciate investment property over 27.5 years at the rate of 3.636 percent per year. That means that for a $200K property, you depreciate $7,272 per year against your active income. In the beginning, seven thousand dollars might not seem like a big deal, but as you add more investment properties and start making more money, depreciation becomes an insanely useful tool to not only make and build wealth but to keep it.

Cash Flow

If you are the obsessing type, cash flow is the muse that will inspire some incredible dreams. Every month, the cash flow coming in from your investment properties is money you didn't have to spend any time creating. Then the rents from your investments come in, and this sweet cash flow makes a huge difference when payments such as your mortgage, insurance, and taxes come due.

Cash flow is a great tool and the one that I've found new investors fixate on above all others. That's fine. Personally, I won't buy an investment that doesn't generate cash flow. As an investor, you always want to make sure you can cover the costs of all of your monthly expenses and still have money left over each month.

Do not create highly optimistic cash flow projections without allocating money for expenses like maintenance and cap-X (capital expenditures: high-dollar stuff like the roof, windows, and HVAC). If you are going to use property management services, even in the future, know that these expenses will typically run you between 7 and 10 percent per month of gross rents. I also like to include reserves—at minimum, a few thousand dollars per property held for issues that will come up over time, as well as monthly reserves held back for the future. Stuff happens so prepare for it.

At first, your cash flow will not change much for you financially. If you buy one or two single-family homes, you might net a few hundred dollars a month after all the expenses and reserves are subtracted. That's not really that earth-shattering, and certainly won't change your family's financial future. However, as you grow your portfolio to ten properties that are creating the same $200 to $300 per month in net cash flow, you now have a total of $2,000 to $3,000 per month. If you incur a large expense on a property, it's much easier to cover the cost of that repair because you have a larger number of properties creating more monthly cash flow from the rents. This dramatically helps you cover expenses, such as maintenance and repairs, when they come up rather than having to dip into reserves.

As your principal is paid down, or you focus on paying off one property in your portfolio, your cash flow can rise dramatically. But please note the choice of paying off your properties is not to be taken lightly. If you are in a growth and scaling mode and want to add properties to your portfolio, paying your properties down doesn't make sense.

Back to the Numbers

Let's say your goal is to create $10K a month in passive income, which will more than cover most W-2 jobs. That gives you a whole lot of personal freedom to decide if you want to stay in your job or double down in real estate. You just located, negotiated, and added your tenth property to your portfolio. Using Midwest numbers, the average value of those middle-of-the-road rental properties is $150K to $200K per door. So your portfolio value is around $1.5M to $2.0M. Well done, future real estate multimillionaire! With just a little time, focus, and perseverance, you are well on your way to creating $10K per month and the incredible life we keep talking about.

If you have ten properties and the average rent per door is about $1,400, you are receiving $14K per month in gross rents. You are netting $250 per door after all of your expenses, including the PITI (Principal, Interest, Taxes, Insurance) as well as some money you are setting aside for reserves, property management, and maintenance. Your total monthly cash flow is $2,500 per month.

Every month, you begin paying the entire net cash flow on the lowest principal balance of the ten mortgages you have. Let's assume for a second that you owe $120K on a thirty-year mortgage with an interest rate of 3.5 percent. Paying $2,500 down per month would roughly pay the rest of that mortgage off in less than five years. With that paid off, you come away with the entire $1,400 monthly rent, grossly increasing your cash flow on that property.

This process of paying properties down takes some time, but the snowball effect of making regular monthly payments on all but one property is exponential. You add the additional $1,400 per month in net cash flow, and you can pay the next property off that much faster. Some people love to pay their properties off so they have no debt. Others love to refinance over and over (tax-free) and take home large chunks of money that way. To achieve the goal of $10K per month, you could take these ten properties and pay them off or continue to acquire additional units using leverage.

The bottom line with cash flow is versatility. You can utilize it in many ways that will create monthly income for you over time. Don't get overly optimistic when you do your numbers, though, and have some money set aside for repairs. Build momentum in your real estate business, and enjoy the cash flow and freedom that comes from it.

Leverage

One plus one is not two in real estate leverage. You can pay far less than the value of the real estate you want to purchase and use leverage, or loans, to cover the rest. Leverage allows you to use other people's money, such as a private lender, a friend, a bank, or a credit union. We will get into the specifics of the different types of lenders in a moment, but know that your lender can cover the vast majority of the total cost of the purchase you are making.

Let's say you have $200K to invest in real estate, and you are working on a plan for how you want to invest. If you want to consider a $200K rental property purchase and don't use leverage, you would be responsible for paying the entire $200K to close the deal. In most cases with an investment property, a lender will cover up to about 80 percent of the purchase price. That means that to buy and control that $200K investment, you only need $40K down to close the deal. That leaves you with $160K in cash to invest in other properties. Using that same $200K to invest in real estate, you would now have the down payment (minus reserves and closing costs) for five properties of the same value. You just went from owning one house to owning five with that same $200K investment. And from controlling $200K worth of real estate to controlling $1M.

The higher the leverage in your portfolio, however, the more overall risk you take on because with higher leverage, you have less equity in your properties. Let's say you own those ten properties at $150K a door for a total portfolio value of $1.5M. If you had 70 percent leverage on that portfolio, your mortgage balance would be $1.05M. That also would mean you have just shy of $500K in equity. Increase that leverage to 80 percent of the house value and you owe $1.2M and have only $300K in equity. On the other hand, the higher the leverage you have, the higher your return on your cash down payment, because it takes less of your own money to make that cash back from your investment. You receive your return on your investment as you collect rent and net the difference between the rent and the PITI. You also can use all of the additional real estate facets to your benefit such as depreciation and principal pay-down.

Leverage is both a tool to scale your portfolio and a long-term philosophy for you to cultivate as you figure out how you want to operate your real estate business. Give leverage a thoughtful amount of your time as the higher the leverage, the more long-term risk you have in that portfolio. Unless you have a sizable reserve in cash in case something were to happen, like a downturn in the market or higher vacancy, you may need more liquidity than you have at that moment. Long term, I prefer to carry much less than 80 percent leverage in my portfolio, say 50 to 60 percent max. I prefer a balance, using leverage to scale while also having substantial equity in case I want to refinance, take money out, or there's a change in the market—the equity allows me to sell or change out investments without having to bring my own cash to do it.

Principal Pay-Down

Imagine you own a property and the tenant has occupied it and is paying the rent. They are now covering the mortgage payment that you owe on that home (or at least they should be). Every single month when the rent is paid and you make your mortgage payment, a portion of that payment goes to interest on the loan and another portion goes to pay the taxes and insurance on the property. The remaining portion of the payment goes to the principal of the loan. That means every single month, the principal balance of the mortgage, or what you owe, goes down.

The amortization of your loan, or the timeline you pay it over, is usually fifteen, twenty, or thirty years for an investment loan. That means the entire balance of the loan is paid for during that time. The lower the number of years, the higher the mortgage payment, but the less interest you will pay over that time. If you have a goal of paying off just a few properties in a short period of time, a fifteen-year mortgage that has you paying that principal down with extra payments might be the way to go.

Whichever mortgage length you choose, the principal, or total amount you owe, goes down each month. Coupled with potential appreciation of the property (its value going up) or depreciation of the property (writing off a portion of its value to lower taxes), using the leverage to control a property instead of all of your cash makes real estate a wealth-creating and life-changing opportunity. In the beginning, you won't pay down much of the mortgage, and that's okay. But as time passes, all of these amazing real estate tools have a larger impact, giving you that many more options of what to do next. Will you pay the property off and generate even more cash flow, or refinance and take chunks of money out tax-free? Both provide awesome results and dramatically increase your income and your ability to live the life you want.

The Primary Types of Real Estate Investments

There are numerous ways you can build a real estate investment business. However, here we are going to lay out the three basic models so that you can understand their differences and discover which business type most excites you. There are no wrong answers, but deciding on one initial path and executing it with one hundred percent of your focus is crucial to your success.

The three types of investment used by most people I know are buy and hold, fix and flip, and wholesaling. Each of these has its advantages and disadvantages, so let's take a look at them one by one. Over the course of my real estate career, I have been involved with all of them, but I keep coming back to one, which

I wish I had stuck with over the others—the holy grail of buy-and-hold investing.

Buy and Hold

Once you buy a property, make sure the renovation is done well (if any renovations are needed), keep the property in top shape, manage the property, receive rents, and settle in for a long period of ownership. Some people like to hold properties for shorter time frames, such as five to seven years. One of my friends, who owns thousands of doors, will only purchase what he wants to hold "forever." Buying and holding is the slow game of building a massive real estate portfolio and wealth in real estate.

When you buy and hold a property, you aren't reselling, so you don't have to go through the process of finding a buyer, then finding, purchasing, and renovating another house. When you fix and flip a property, every time you sell that house, you have to buy another one to make money from it and endure the entire process over and over. Alternatively, every property you add to your buy-and-hold portfolio goes into the long-term plan to create wealth, using all the tools we just talked about earlier in this chapter. With the buy-and-hold business model, you can create a real estate portfolio that will "cash flow" every month and eventually, as you scale it, cover and then far exceed what you need to live.

As you begin to underwrite buy-and-hold properties, pay particular attention to the cost of the mortgage, the rents that you can get, and the difference between them. Always include the cost of a property management company as you will most likely not want to handle management long term, or build a company that does it for you. Check that the cash flow between what the mortgage costs you and the rents you receive is enough to keep you comfortable as you create both short-term safety in that investment and build the overall cash flow that you want long term.

Beyond the monthly cash flow, as that portfolio is paid off over time you will have a growing amount of equity. Just in the past year or two, I have had multiple friends pay off the entire mortgage on their personal home with the equity from a tax-free refinance of their real estate portfolios. In addition, most of them didn't see their mortgage payment change much compared to what they were paying before they took that tax-free gold through refinancing. Typically in these scenarios, they had owned their investment properties for a number of years, so their interest rates were higher than the current market rate at that time. The value of their properties had also increased substantially, so there was a lot of equity within their portfolio. By refinancing, they were able to take out money tax-free, reset their loans, and even lock in the current mortgage rate that was usually better than what they had before. Buy-and-hold investing has created incredible lifestyles for many people I know, and it's what we, in our business, are in the process of creating for ourselves, too.

Just this year, we will add nearly seventy new construction doors to our real estate portfolio. Those seventy doors will be valued at around $8.5M, with roughly 20 percent equity or $1.68M. Buy-and-hold investing will change your life; it just takes time for it to grow and scale. Start with your first property or a goal of one or two properties in a year. Learn at a small scale so that as you begin to add properties at a faster rate, you can operate with the confidence and understanding of the lessons you learned early on. Gain a better understanding of what you like to buy and hold long term. And begin to build a team around you who understand what properties you want and know how to buy and renovate them. Finally, find a bank that wants to finance your homes when they're completed and occupied by a great tenant. You don't need to move fast to build wealth, but you do have to take action, learn from your mistakes, and continue to pursue the goals and the vision you have created.

Fix and Flip

When I first got into real estate, I was solely focused on buying and holding for the long term. However, I soon encountered other interested investors who would gladly pay me the entire value of a ready-to-go property after we would buy it and renovate it. It was a great deal for us because we would make the difference between the initial buying price plus renovations and what we sold it for. As investors, they didn't have to learn about and develop all the systems and teams to buy, renovate, and manage the projects. Instead, they would purchase the house completed and get a great return based on the price of the property and the rents they would receive.

I love taking the worst property in a great area and bringing it back to life. It's fun to design what the property will look like and envision a happy family making it their home once we complete the renovation. We grew our business around buying and renovating homes, holding some, and selling others to investors from all over the world who want to do the same thing for themselves.

Fix and flip is a tremendous opportunity to make large amounts of cash if you build your systems and invest wisely. You need to identify properties priced under market value that need work. The money you make is the spread between what you purchased the property for (plus the cost of renovations and the cost of the sale), and what it will sell for when you have completed it. As an example, if you purchase a house for $250K, put $50K into it, spend $20K for closing costs and realtor fees, and sell for $360K, your spread in the deal is $40K. Having bought, renovated, and sold nearly 700 homes in the last six years, I can tell you they don't always go that way.

There is a saying in real estate that your money is made on the "buy," and that is mostly accurate. Buying properties with the intention to renovate them and sell them can be very lucrative, but you must have the process and management set up. First, you underwrite the property based on the location and what the value of the completely renovated property should bring based on comparable sold properties near yours. Make sure you work with another investor who knows the area or a realtor who is investor-savvy until you are clear on how to pull comparable sales and set pricing for your investments. Don't get overly optimistic when you purchase the property by expecting more money than you can realistically get when selling it or expecting lower renovation costs than it requires. Either or both of those false hopes will immediately put you in a bad situation even before you have started the renovation or listed the home for sale.

Next, estimate the cost of construction in the design and renovation phase to bring the property up to the level of quality that will result in getting the price you expect to sell it for. You may want to hire contractors for some amazing design work specific to your style, but the intention is to make the property interesting to the greatest number of people possible so that you will have the best potential of selling it for what you want to get. Once you've purchased the property, you must manage the renovation and construction portion carefully. Sign a rock-solid contract with your contractor, even if it means working with your real estate attorney to make sure the contract is clear and the timeline and cost are understood by all parties. Keep clear communications with your contractor and make regular reviews of your project during construction to ensure it is going to be delivered on time, on budget, and at the level of quality you agreed on.

Once the project is completed, bring your realtor in if you aren't listing the property yourself. Have professional pictures taken, consider staging the home if other comparable properties are staged, and price the property right where it should be based on those comparable sales. Fix-and-flip investing is a great strategy and one I have personally engaged in for nearly my entire real estate career. However, fix and flipping at any scale is a grind. Seriously consider if you want to have to go find another property every month to replace the one you just sold—funding your deals, managing contractors, and enduring the sales process of coordinating, listing, negotiating, and selling your properties each time. You may just find that level of effort isn't worth it and may want to buy and hold instead, building your wealth one property at a time. Or you can create a plan that balances selling off a few fix-and-flip properties to create short-term income while you scale, holding the best properties that fit your portfolio criteria long term.

Wholesaling

Wholesaling is an incredible tool to create short-term income, but it can also pull your attention away from your long-term wealth goals. In essence, with wholesaling, you find a seller of a property, put that property under contract, and then sell the option for that contract for more than your purchase price. Often this looks like some form of marketing as you receive and pursue inbound leads of people who want to sell their properties. They are usually in some kind of distress or crisis, such as a recent death in the family, divorce, job loss, or a move to another state. Usually, the property needs some work, from a small paint and carpet job to a full property renovation. The wholesaler will walk that seller through how best to get their home sold and put the property under contract. Then, either using an option contract or closing on the property and reselling it, they will sell that property to an investor who wants to buy it to hold or to fix and flip.

I've purchased hundreds of homes over the years from wholesalers, and the work and service they provide are extremely valuable. Working with amazing wholesalers enabled us to focus more on dialing in what we buy in acquisitions, renovating those properties, and helping investors and homeowners purchase a great home. We would have had to create an in-house, direct-to-seller acquisition team and process if it were not for the great wholesalers we worked with.

Several investor friends of mine have built incredibly profitable companies using this method of investing. Typically, they will take and invest large parts of their short-term cash from the wholesaling business in other real estate such as apartment deals or even portfolios of rental properties. Just like a fix-and-flip business, wholesaling requires that you go and find new sellers, write new contracts, and cycle through this process over and over to create the next month's revenue.

Many new investors get into wholesaling without understanding the real estate business, and that can create serious chaos. Problems can arise from not knowing how to legally put together contracts, missing the next steps once a property is under contract, selling without a clear title, or even not knowing how to sell the property. Learn and understand the pricing of a property and sell it for an amount that's based on comparable sales, the renovation costs, and what the investors you sell to typically pay. I've personally encountered many novice wholesalers who simply didn't understand how the process works or how to price a property. As a result, they hurt the seller who really needed to sell and wasted our time as the investor/buyer. If you decide to try wholesaling, take it seriously. Use legally dialed-in contracts, and don't put homes under contract that you aren't sure you can sell.

Wholesaling is often a focus of new investors because they think it is the easiest and least costly real estate business to get into. Any business or endeavor will take an investment of your time, focus, and even money, so base your decision about how you will start not just on your perception of short-term ease but for the long-term outcome. Don't make money or inexperience an excuse for not pursuing the real business you want to be in now. All the funding, mentors, answers, and models are already out there for you to create what you want today.

Creating Your Property Buy Box

There are just as many types of properties you can invest in as there are colors in that perfect Crayola crayon box. Houses come in many shapes, sizes, areas, ages, and more. It's imperative as you begin to decide where you will put your investing focus to create what is called a "buy box" for your investments. Your buy box sets the parameters for what kinds of properties you will invest in based on criteria you've decided up-front. Operating your real estate business with a predetermined set of rules takes out the emotion when it's time to decide on whether to pull the trigger. A property either fits the criteria of homes I want to buy—fits in my buy box—or it doesn't.

When I talk with new investors, I like to focus their attention on a few key criteria. I want them to consider and determine the before-repair price range of properties they want to buy, the ARV (After-Repair Value) price range, the age of the home, the size and number of bedrooms, the type of area where the home is located, the style of home, and the exit they are planning for that investment. I enter each of these as bullet points in a spreadsheet along with the investor's decisions. This is their buy box. Its defined parameters allow an investor to make a much faster decision without feeling frustration or anxiety over whether a property is a good deal. The buy box is also easy to share and can become the foundation for training someone else on your team what to buy, where to buy, and how much to pay.

The price you are willing to pay greatly depends on your plan for the property, your level of risk tolerance, your exit plan (if you are keeping it or when you plan to sell it), and the return you want to make on the property. If you are buying and holding the property and don't mind having some money left in the property when you are done, you might not mind paying more for the property than if you were buying to flip it.

If you are planning to buy, renovate, and sell a house for a profit on the MLS, determine a minimum for what you are willing to make after all expenses. In my own business, every time we would deviate from what we were willing to make on a property, we regretted not holding the line and passing for a better property. Doing the same work for less money isn't fun. Even worse, bringing money to the closing table after a real estate renovation, because the house sells for less than you have in it, is an unpleasant experience. I've paid to sell a house and it sucks.

After-Repair Value (ARV) is determined by looking at properties near the subject property that are similar in size and condition, and seeing what they sold for. Our buy box ARV range for properties in our market is typically between $100K and $300K. That means every house we consider buying would be worth up to $300K after we bought it, renovated it, and completed the project. Even if there is a deal that could bring in $100K in potential profit, if the ARV is above the threshold of $300K, the deal is an automatic no. The deal has to fit in our buy box, or we don't buy the house. We aren't going to deviate from the locations we know, the type of properties we renovate, or the price range we are comfortable investing in.

Funding Your Investments

I've lived by a saying for a long time: "Don't make money your problem; make your problem your problem." This couldn't be truer than when you begin thinking about how you will fund a real estate purchase, short or long term. Yes, you need to work on having good credit, hold back some reserves for your investment properties, and cash in your personal savings account. But know that if you have a good plan, there are many ways you can put a deal together without having great credit or hundreds of thousands of dollars in cash. What you do need is the desire to create awesome opportunities—and the willingness to figure out solutions that work.

Although you could create many funding or financing structures, there are a few very effective ways to think about funding and scaling your investments. The absolute simplest way is to utilize bank financing by putting down about 20 percent cash on each of the properties you purchase. Start a relationship with a local credit union or community bank versus working with one of the big banks. The experience is completely different because community bankers and credit union bankers tend to have a better understanding of real estate investments and a desire to build real and lasting relationships. Once I understood this difference, I moved all of my real estate investments and personal and business banking to my favorite institutions; the experience, efficiency, and products were dramatically better for me as an investor.

The other reason to start a community bank relationship is that even if you use a mortgage broker for your first few investment properties, you can only secure so many loans like the one you have for your primary residence where you live. These mortgages have to meet specific guidelines, are packaged, and are then usually sold to Fannie Mae and Freddie Mac, which oversee trillions of dollars of loans. You can only have up to ten of these loans, and it's hard to get up to even that number given the complex underwriting and the reserves they require. Community banks and credit unions have a different set of criteria, based on you as the investor, your total financial picture, what your goals are, and the relationship you have created. Explain what you want to create, lay out your vision to the banker you have chosen, and ask what it will take to get their help so that you can be great partners together for the long term.

Community banks and credit unions have lending caps; the smaller ones are usually at least a few million dollars per customer. You can even ask for what is called a guidance line, which ensures that as long as you keep buying these kinds of rental properties, they will automatically approve up to $2M of such loans at 80 percent LTV (loan to value). So, in this instance, even with an average value of properties at $200K, you could acquire over ten properties before having to ask for more money from the bank, and you'll be able to streamline the acquisitions of your investments.

Funding your deals using private, or hard, money to acquire and renovate a property, even if you choose to hold it for a short period, can be really advantageous. Private money might come from an investor, a business, or even a loan from your friend's self-directed IRA account. Hard money is often provided by a local investor or business that will lend money on real estate deals solely based on the numbers of a particular deal. Whatever the source of money, this becomes your "bank" that lends you the money to purchase and renovate a property. Once that renovation is complete, you take the property to your new credit union or bank and have them refinance it. I've done tens of millions in deals with both of these types of loans, and they are very effective for short-term funding.

Talk with someone at your local title company or an attorney to get professional help creating the right contract, which will keep both you and your lender safe. An agreement should be spelled out clearly so that everyone understands what's happening, including what you and the lender are responsible for, how much is due, and when the loan should be repaid. Even though this type of loan is typically a little more expensive, it's also way more flexible, provides faster funding than a bank, and is more asset-based. Growing a relationship with these short-term lenders and using these loans can help you make cash offers and close on properties faster and more easily than your competitors using bank funding. These lenders will become a part of your go-to team, which also includes people at the banks and credit unions. Being able to bring hard money to the table will make you strong, agile, and effective so that you can close quickly on the front end of your deals, but you'll always want to have a bank or credit union that wants to serve as the long-term lender for your investments.

Creating Your Investment Vision

When you find yourself daydreaming, what type of investment property are you fantasizing about buying? Are you investing in the urban core because you want to change the face of that part of the city? Or high-end homes in the suburbs? Are you designing and selling a few fix-and-flip properties or building a flipping machine that buys, renovates, and sells hundreds of homes a year? Wherever you find your daydreams take you over and over is the direction you should go in as you begin to build out your investing plan. You will know it's the right direction because you won't be able to think about anything else.

Write down what your next steps are as far as you can see them. What relationships will you need to forge to take your next steps? You may need to seek out lenders, attorneys, real estate agents, and maybe even a mentor or coach who understands and is doing what you want to do. Lay out your plan, and ask for feedback from the team of professionals you are building. At every step, understand that challenges will come up, and expect and welcome them. Know that problems are a part of your learning, a part of the journey, and will always be a part of your business. A good deal of your success will depend on understanding this and on making decisions that might be uncomfortable—the same way creating a vision of what your business will be in the future can be uncomfortable because you don't have experience and knowledge yet. Embrace it. Love the process of discovering your business and yourself.

CHAPTER 8

THE NO QUITTERS' SECRET WEAPONS: YOUR WHY, IMPERFECT ACTION, AND GO-GIVER MENTORS

An incredibly defined and compelling "why" creates clarity. The clarity you need to experience the most extraordinary moments in your life. No matter what difficulties you encounter, challenges you face, or roadblocks you must overcome, no problem is too great or too difficult to solve if you have a why. Accomplishing your why fuels you, gives you purpose, and grounds you in any situation. It guides you back to the reason you are on the planet and allows you to evaluate how solving the mountain-sized problem before you is tied to the life experience you want to have.

Not having a clear why creates the opposite effect: a lack of focus, wandering, hoping, regret, and deeply misaligned feelings, actions, and outcomes. When problems arise, you won't have a big enough reason to keep going. You won't want to get back up because you won't have conviction that what is beyond that problem is something so important that nothing can stop you. When your why is blurry, like a photograph that would be fantastic but is just ever so slightly out of focus, your drive and determination will fluctuate. Some days, you may be excited to work toward what you think you want, and some days it will seem impossible to find the energy or passion to do the job.

A massively powerful and motivating why can take many forms. There isn't a right or wrong why. However, I've found the most compelling visions of purpose go beyond ourselves as individuals. It might be getting a manned mission to Mars as Elon Musk has mentioned. Or winning basketball championships like Michael Jordan. Or changing the financial trajectory of your family's legacy by putting three generations of your family through college. It may be saving an animal species from extinction. Or transforming a neighborhood, city, or even country from poor or war-stricken to more prosperous or peaceful. The most compelling whys impact the most people and create the greatest positive change in the world.

More Than a Flight

From an early age, I was encouraged by my parents to go on mission trips with our church, both within and beyond the

United States. It never failed, whether I helped build a house in Texas with hundreds of kids from all over the country, or a small orphanage in the inner city of St. Louis, or a church one hundred yards from the soaring stalks of a huge sugarcane field in Venezuela (shoveling and making concrete bucket by bucket), these life experiences had a lasting impact on me. Although every time my intention on these missions was to help other people in a big way, after each trip it felt like somehow I had received more than I had given. I gained more in experience, gratitude, and appreciation than I could ever give back.

It was in that spirit a few years ago that I settled into my seat on an outbound flight headed to Port-au-Prince, Haiti. Like I always do on flights, I engaged with the person next to me to see what kind of interesting conversation might come from it. As the plane rushed down the runway and the pilot somehow maneuvered yet another giant jet with hundreds of people into the air, my conversation with the man sitting next to me unfolded. We began with small talk about how the day was going and how travel had thankfully gone smoothly so far for both of us. About the time the plane crested ten thousand feet, we got to the question, "So what brings you to Haiti?"

Haiti is a powerful dichotomy. The poorest nation in the Western Hemisphere, it is an incredibly beautiful but also incredibly heartbreaking country. The poverty there, the lack of jobs, housing, healthcare, and even food and water, is absolutely devastating for its people. As it turned out, my seatmate, Jared, and I were both headed to Haiti to try to help.

I shared with Jared that a friend of mine had started an orphanage in Haiti, and a small group of philanthropic-minded real estate investors, myself included, were headed there to work at the orphanage and raise money to help more kids. Then Jared shared with me that not only did he do mission work, but he was headed to Haiti to give a speech (in French Creole) because he had established one of just a few nonprofits to be nationally recognized among the thousands in Haiti. His organization had not only helped many orphans but created schools for more kids in the community and many jobs for people who were desperate for any way to make a living and care for their families.

As we felt the plane begin to descend into Port-au-Prince, Jared made me an offer. "I tell you what, Nathan, if you think what we have going on in Haiti sounds interesting, you should come to Honduras and see what we have going on there." And as I watched him confidently walk off the gangway, I said, "I will take you up on that, Jared!" Then I wished him well on his speech, and we headed into the small but insanely bustling confusion of Port-au-Prince International Airport.

Little did Jared expect that I would book flights and travel out to meet him in Tegucigalpa, Honduras, just six weeks later. There I observed firsthand one of the most incredible missions, orphanages, and group of people driven to change the world that I'd ever seen or heard of. Thanks to Jared's vision and his organization Mission Lazarus, they have created incredible trade schools teaching leather making and cabinetry to young men and women while also continuing their regular education. The orphanage was led by the wonderful women, who showed immense love and care to these kids in their most dire and difficult moments of loss. He also founded an organic and fair trade coffee farm selling excellent coffee, and he employed and led dozens of Hondurans to help him carry out this beautifully executed vision. As for me, I experienced a new understanding of how compelling a life-changing why can be.

Jared is the most impactful, mission-minded, yet entrepreneurially driven person I've ever met. His why is the outgrowth of his deeply held religious beliefs. These inspire his desire to help everyone he meets. No matter what he is doing or where he is on the planet, he genuinely wants and works to help make the lives of the people he encounters better. As you wrestle with defining the why in your life, remember that whether your vision of purpose comes from a religious perspective, a passion, a life experience, or just a goal to make life better for others, we all have the power to do extraordinary things and have an extraordinary impact on the world.

Life is far more important and precious than fame, a million dollars in the bank, or a fancy house. Living a truly exceptional life means taking the time required to lay out not only what you want to experience in your life, but how you will positively impact the people and world around you. Invest the time now to create that clear vision so it becomes the powerful why that motivates you to take massive action. This why, chosen with care and intention, will sustain your momentum over time, even when you encounter complications or frustrations along the way. You are put on the planet not just to live and breathe, but to take this gift of life and fulfill a purpose and to make lasting contributions that extend far beyond yourself.

Build an Extraordinary Why

Imagine jumping into your vehicle that's packed to the brim, your family all settled in with seatbelts fastened, ready to go on a memorable trip you've been thinking about for some time. All of your luggage is packed as neatly as the shapes in a game of Tetris. Your favorite road-trip munchies are within easy reach. You turn the key over and the engine starts. But, at that moment, you realize that something is completely off. A wave of anxiety almost paralyzes you. Somehow you planned every detail of what to pack, who was going, and when you wanted to leave, but didn't select the exact location you were headed for or plan what you would do once you got there.

Somehow in life, it seems we spend copious amounts of time and energy on things that don't make much difference or worse things we don't want or care about. In reality, we could have put that same energy into things that matter, into what we do want. Have a positive focus and be proactive in deciding what you want to experience and in taking the steps to accomplish it.

Without a clear and deeply fulfilling why, your effort in business and in your life will have less impact. We all deeply desire a why that connects every aspect of our lives to the core of who we are. A why gives us integrity, because we are always working to be true to our purpose. As your why unfolds and you come to realize it includes positive outcomes for others, you will feel excitement that your purpose extends beyond yourself.

Sometimes when we are first trying to discover our why, we can feel incredible pressure or anxiety to "get it right." Instead of stressing, start by thinking of something that brings you real happiness, and start your exploration of purpose from a positive and powerful state. Feel the excitement, and allow your imagination to bring you to what you are called to do.

I recommend starting with the concrete, filling in specific details of the life you want and then expanding out to consider the larger opportunities and ideas that extend beyond you. Take a breath—maybe even close your eyes for a moment—and imagine yourself living an extraordinary life right now. Where are you living? Are you living near the coastline in California, in a condo in the bustling heart of Brooklyn, or on a sprawling ranch in Montana? Feel the special energy of this incredible place. Next, paint a picture of your home. What does it look like? What is the color of your front door? How does it feel to open the door and walk into the house? What do you see? Is it cozy or expansive, bright or muted, full of antiques or modern furniture? Now write down in crystal-clear detail what you imagined. This is the first step in your plan to bring you to a place of fulfillment, safety, joy, and purpose in your life.

The second step is to imagine the work you will spend time and effort pursuing—work that you love, that you are passionate about, and that brings you energy. *You* decide what days you will work and how often you take days off. What will you do with your time away from work? Play golf, go for a bike ride, or take the kids to the park? Whatever you want to do, imagine you have created the time and space to do it. What about your work environment? Do you have a large team or a small and dynamic office staff? Are you working a lot, or maybe just a few hours a week? Over the years, I've gone from dreaming of hustling and working insane hours to a wanting to spend much less time on work that is, nonetheless, highly profitable, awesome, and engaging. Your preferences may well change over time, and that's okay.

Write down all the details you have imagined about your perfect work life. Include what your position is, how many hours you are working a week, and how much money you make. Concentrate on how it feels to be successful in your work and doing what you love. Allow yourself to feel and experience that fully and record that feeling in your journal. Just because you haven't built that company yet doesn't mean you can't begin to experience success every day as you work toward that goal.

Now, envision your family life. Imagine spending time with your family and friends that is purposeful and stress-free. What does your family enjoy doing together, where, how often? What about family trips? Where are you headed? You are able to afford to go on that road trip to the mountains or take the family to the beach. Now think about your friends who are dear to you. How will you enjoy their company, in your spacious home, taking trips together, enjoying fun hobbies? Your family and friends give you energy. Allow yourself to be fully present with whoever you are with and whatever you are doing together. Of course, I want you to record the details you saw and feelings you had while imagining the contentment of sharing your beautiful life with people you love.

You are doing an incredible job honing and shaping every piece of your extraordinary life.

The big picture begins to take shape as you start to clearly see and inspect each aspect of your new life. Embrace the process.

You are ready to think about the positive outcomes you want to create for others. Who would you like to help? What kind of impact would you like to have? In what area? Do you want to help high school students go to college or improve the environment or provide housing for seniors? What would it take to bring that idea for change to reality? The beginning stages of defining a powerful why that extends beyond you as an individual can be frustrating. You may have a sense of the impact you want to make, but it is not perfectly clear how to accomplish it, or thinking about and working toward it is not yet creating the experience you want it to. That's totally normal. Write down your thoughts, begin to allow yourself to believe you can make this incredible impact, and continue coming back to strategize and refine your vision.

Be patient. Continue to apply a deeper level of focus and intention than you ever have before. As you put forth this new effort, things will slowly come to fruition and begin to manifest and grow over time. If you are like me, it still won't feel like things are happening fast enough. I wanted to see it all come together right away. Alas, just like building a business or learning any new skill, creating and cultivating your why is a long game. But having an incredible impact on others is worthy of your focus and determination long term and will yield more reward than you can even imagine.

Sustaining Your Why over Time

There are many books out there about creating a vision and planning what you want to do and how you want to use your time. Most books I've run across are missing a key element—how to connect the real and profound result you are looking for with the specific day-to-day actions that will produce it. You need both a vision and a plan for execution, but they have to be linked. You may have planned a daily morning routine, but if those activities are not aligned with the goals and life you are seeking, your daily effort will not produce the result. We must seamlessly connect the vision we create with an effective daily practice to accomplish it.

Linking my why to my daily practice starts with my specific morning routine. I'm not going to tell you what time you should get up; just decide when, be consistent, and get up. Hal Elrod's book, *Miracle Morning*, and James Clear's *Atomic Habits* have both given me tools I use every day in my own life. Hal writes about having components to his morning routine, and I used his blueprint to create what works well for me. My day is best started with ten minutes of guided meditation using the "Waking Up" app by Sam Harris. Meditation is not about being "good at it;" it's about spending time sitting with your thoughts to learn about you and grow. I'm not sure if anyone starting out feels they're "good" at meditation, so don't let that keep you from continuing this practice when you first get into it.

After I've sat in meditation, I open the pages of my journal and write out at least three things that I am grateful for. No matter how the week or day is going, this puts me into a state of gratitude and appreciation. This is the right mental state to dig into the why I have created and evaluate the next steps I need to take to continue working on it. I review and write out what my day looks like and what I need to do to keep my activity in line with my vision—my why. I ask myself, *What are the activities I am working on today that will help me accomplish this incredible life I want to live?* If you aren't spending the majority of your time working toward that goal, then are you really working to bring that why, that life, to fruition? I don't believe you will accomplish much of any magnitude without focused activity in alignment with the result you want. Choose how you spend your time with focused care and thought.

My morning journal time also includes reviewing what my goals are for the week, the month, and the current quarter. It's important to not just check off the boxes next to the goals you've laid out to accomplish. The point is to review and evaluate whether every single thing you are spending your time on is effectively helping you to accomplish your goal. Also ask yourself if the tasks you have set are enjoyable and what you want to do. The more aligned your daily work is with what you like to do and what your goals are, the more effective your time is and the more sustainable that work is over time. Don't expect to continue to do something you hate or are not good at doing. Instead, do what you like and do well, keep doing it over time, and believe that this is a sustainable plan. Remember, the work you are doing, regardless of whether it brings in a lot of money, will not by itself create an incredible life.

After I've completed my journal time, I open up my tunes, crank something I am in the mood for that morning, and do a short but high-intensity workout. This is not my workout for the day, just a mind-body connection. I love the mental clarity that comes from exercise. The kettlebells are in a corner of my office, waiting for me to swing them every time I walk in. I'll usually combine some kettlebells, pushups, sit-ups, and squats. I believe that getting your body moving, getting into a powerful state, is all part of starting your day and setting yourself up for success.

Some people love to read in the morning, but reading hasn't become part of my a.m. routine. I typically listen to about two audio books a month during travel time or between other things I'm doing. I listen to business, leadership, and self-development podcasts as well as books while I drive. There's nothing like windshield education—learning and getting fired up while driving to an exciting lunch appointment or business meeting.

As I mentioned in chapter 6, each quarter, I decide on one personal, one family, and one business goal. Some of my past goals have included drinking measurably less alcohol, getting consistent with meditation if I haven't been, and even committing to train twelve hours a week at my MMA gym in preparation for a cage fight. For my family, I've focused on weekly one-on-one time with my kids and wife as well as a weekly discussion of family budgeting and saving and how that matches are family's yearly targets. For business goals, I have worked on finding a coach to help our team with challenges, and digging into a specific problem by connecting with the people on our team who are closest to it. Consistency is key for the practice of goal setting. No matter what, each quarter I have three specific goals in each of the three categories. There hasn't been a single thing I've accomplished that I haven't first written down in my journal, and then taken the action I've laid out.

Creating the life you want requires you to choose the specific direction you want to go in and then take action that will move you toward that objective. Nothing in your life will have a great effect or forge a deep connection to what you deeply want without your making the decision to link your activity to your goals. Spend the necessary time to first create your why, and then ask yourself what it will take to make that sustainable over time. This sets you up perfectly for a big-picture plan and the concrete steps to achieve it.

Imperfect Action Is Perfect

As you are creating your plan and setting goals, know that no matter what decisions you make, there will be some that aren't the right ones. Some ideas will fail; sometimes you will wonder what you have gotten yourself into. It's possible that your initial business idea, or the first three, will fail. Statistically, far more businesses fail than succeed. I would know; I was one of those statistics during my first go at real estate more than a decade ago. I had to face the brutal facts of my failures, clarify what I wanted to create, and make a decision as to whether I wanted to take more imperfect action toward the life experience I wanted.

Make no mistake, identifying and taking action can be overwhelming. Just in choosing investment properties there are so many choices. Where geographically will you make your investments? What will the inside of your rentals look like? Don't allow these smaller decisions to become roadblocks. They are simply problems to figure out in a world filled with books, podcasts, and coaches that can help you effectively solve them.

Every new piece of information you absorb and every discovery of what you want or don't want advances you in aligning all of the parts of your life and business with what you want to experience. If you are struggling with how to finance your properties, meet regularly with new bankers. Tell them what you are looking to create and over what period of time, and ask if it is something they would be interested in investing in. If you aren't sure how to comp properties, ask a few top realtors who do the most deals in your market to meet with you. Offer to compensate them, and explain exactly what you need help with and if they would be willing to spend some time helping you learn.

No matter what your goal, you will get 1 percent closer to it every day as you learn, connect, and grow. Some days, it will feel like you took a massive leap in your game plan, and some days you will feel like you went backward. Sometimes you may even feel like you are stuck in the same spot, just running in place. Execute your morning game plan. Review your activity to make sure the connection to your vision, your why is clear. Write out, review, refine, and take the necessary steps every day to build your extraordinary life.

You Do Not Serve Your Business

Your business is built to serve you; you should not be serving the business. You are not a slave to your business or the job you do for your company. Most people believe that being successful demands constant, endless hours of work checking off tasks on a never-ending to-do list. Certainly, creating any business takes time, effort, and patience. But it shouldn't be a never-ending hustle and grind forever. There is an ebb and flow of opportunities. Be intentional in creating space for pursuing your goals in other areas of your life, and allow your team to do their jobs so you can have space. Don't base your business or your life solely on your work; you want to spend time extraordinary things.

When you work, there are always difficult problems to figure out, challenges with partners or staff, and real issues to resolve. This is true whether you work for yourself or for someone else.

The difference is that in your own business you've created a work environment based on the life you want to live and the purpose it brings. A business should produce or do something that you are proud of. The people who work for that business should love what they do and be connected to the mission you have laid out for them as well.

Each step of building your business should purposefully create the life you want to live, giving you the time and financial freedom to do what you want. Over time, your business can dramatically change your life as you go from asking "I hope someday I can . . . ?" to "What would it take for me to be able to . . . ?" Like Yoda says in Star Wars, "Do or do not, there is no try."

Early on in my business, I missed this concept completely. I worked endless hours every week, missing nearly everything I should have done with or for my family, for my health, and for joy. I felt a deep disconnect from the people closest to me while simultaneously being seen in the real estate community as someone who was setting the example for what a real estate investor should be. They were wrong and I was deeply miserable.

I came to realize that my effort in the business, no matter how much money I made, didn't let me live an extraordinary life. It was just work. As I started to sort out how I felt and what my daily experience in my work was like, I realized how much I didn't enjoy my days because of everything I was responsible for doing. Once I started to open my mind to what I wanted my daily experience to be like, everything started to change. I was less afraid and more empowered to ask for help doing tasks I didn't want to do. That delegation created a bond with the person I was asking for help; they usually wanted to help take those tasks off my plate and felt more connected to our mission as I shared how to do those things and trained them to take them over.

As more of those tasks were no longer my responsibility, I suddenly found more free time in my schedule to do things in my business, with my family, and in my personal life that I wanted to do. I started with blocking off Thursday afternoons in my calendar. Giving myself permission to create free time in my life was part of the experience of building a company. It is built to serve me, not the other way around.

I purposefully have a lot of different hobbies that both challenge me and bring me joy. Creating more time enabled me to come back to these old passions and to seek out and learn new ones. The better I got at asking for help, delegating things that I didn't love doing, and holding responsibility only for the most important tasks and things that I wanted to do, the better my life became in every way. I was only doing what I wanted to both at work and in my personal life.

Your purpose and vision in life and business will attract others. As your why becomes clearer and your plan is laid out, people who resonate with your vision will want to be a part of your team and help you bring it to life. Your purpose will become more connected to leading and helping others so they can also experience joy and success in their own work and life experiences. My why took on even more meaning as I realized that part of it was to help my team by giving them a better and deeper understanding of how money works along with a basic financial education. My partner and I weren't going to help grow wealth for our clients and for ourselves without also helping our team to do the same.

Give the Gift of You

Every person has the opportunity to have a deep and lasting positive effect on someone else. I believe we are more fulfilled when we experience a better life, but we have more joy while helping others. When I've suggested this concept to new investors or coaching students of mine, they are often perplexed. They ask: "What could I possibly do to help someone else? I am just getting started." The answer: You can do much more than you can imagine.

In Bob Burg's inspiring book, *The Go-Giver*, he writes, "Your true worth is determined by how much more you give in value than you take in payment." We have the wonderful opportunity to impact others with the talents, perspective, and drive we have right now. Your gift to someone could be as simple as being able to see a solution they might not be able to see because they are too close to the problem. Not only can we help somebody right now, but we don't have to act like someone else, someone who knows it all, to make a huge impact. We are most helpful when we are simply ourselves, willing to share our experiences and our abilities with others.

I have a highly successful friend, Marck, who has been a real estate investor much longer than I have. In fact, not only is he in real estate, he operates in the same market as me, making us direct competitors. Although we regularly offer on the same deals, Marck has been a go-giver over and over to me in my business—he has done this by checking on how we are doing and helping me solve problems he's worked through before. Just because we have had success in our business doesn't mean I don't need help too. I still need someone to be a sounding board, mentor, and guide while working through challenges. Marck has had a massive positive influence on me and how I've run my business, giving me his time to work through challenges we've both had, even though he had no reason to help. No matter where you are, what your business looks like, or how successful you are at the moment, you can help someone.

Most new investors I meet see how incredible their life could potentially be but have not yet put in the work to create their vision, find their why, and make a plan. Often someone who's asked to go to coffee or lunch with me to benefit from my experience has no idea what they want to know or ask me. I used to accept any request for a coffee or lunch meeting after my experience with Rob because he changed my life, and I wanted to do the same for others. But so many times, people showed up unprepared, not clear on the help they needed, asking me to essentially create their business for them, not having made a start or done any research. So if you are the mentor, it's okay to ask the person who wants your time to put in some work ahead of the meeting and provide you with a specific question or problem they need advice about. This is just the flip side of my earlier advice when asking for someone's time and attention: show up prepared. Time is valuable and you must understand that, respect that, and treat others' time that way.

Everyone Needs a Coach

Coaches have influenced who I am for the better in all of my life roles—husband, father, man, human, and of course, business owner. My coaches have been friends, paid consultants, and tactical, specific problem-solvers. I am infinitely further along in my journey toward my vision because of the men and women who have taken their time to help me in more ways than they could imagine.

Coaches in my life have challenged me to see things already present that I was unable to observe without their help. They've asked probing questions I hadn't thought of and helped me break through problems with people, processes, opportunities, and my own attitude. Many times to get past a roadblock, I needed someone else I could trust to sit in the situation with me and work through what was really happening. As I've already shared with you, my partner and I pay to participate in a mastermind group of the highest-achieving real estate investors, where we receive incredible coaching that benefits our company.

When seeking a coach, look for someone who will challenge you, help you, and guide you on your way to creating your incredible life. They should support you in uncovering what path you want to take, in deciding what actions are needed, and making sure those actions are in alignment with the vision of what you ultimately want to accomplish. Pick someone who can see where you want to go and has created their own extraordinary life for themselves. Many people before you have had dreams that seemed impossible to make real. They have encountered problems and challenges, worked through them, and can help you do the same.

Before you start with a coach, it's critical you have a clear picture of what working together will be like. Ask them how much time they will be committing to you each week and each month? Spell out the end result you are looking to get from the time together. If they aren't all-in to help you create what it is you want in your life, they aren't a good fit. Your coach or mentor might require a financial investment that may seem like a large sum of money to you right now. If they have worked with a lot of other people, have a proven track record, and can get you to your goal, how can you *not* afford to invest in that kind of help? I have personally spent hundreds of thousands of dollars on coaching. It's been one hundred percent worth it for the immense positive impact it's had in my personal and business life.

Michael Jordan and Tiger Woods have both had professional coaches who worked through every aspect of their game to help put them, and keep them, at the pinnacle of their sports. Growing a business and being a successful investor is no different; we all need a coach to help us. As you imagine the incredible life you want to live and the successful business you want to own, also keep in mind that you will want and need coaches and mentors along the way who inspire you, check you, and can work through the problems and opportunities that you will continue to encounter as your business and life develop. A coach or mentor who is truly there to help you through each of those phases will be invaluable as you grow.

Creating an extraordinary life means building what you really want, starting from a clear vision of what it will be. The business is meant to serve you and your purpose, so working together with the team that you assemble, create space both to build a successful company and to enjoy life. Spend time with you family and friends and other incredible people who can not only experience that life with you but who you can serve and bless. The more you work at creating and cultivating your why, the clearer it will become, and the more direct the path to create it. Seek out incredible mentors and coaches to help you achieve what you want. Always remember that life is most fulfilling not when you accomplish financial success but when you help others in the process.

CHAPTER 9

NO QUITTERS' DIAGNOSTICS

When I begin with a new coaching student or client, I always ask the question, "What's driving your desire to get into real estate?" I want to really understand what their motivation is beneath the surface of making money or creating a business.

I've found every student, every client, every colleague was drawn to some specific aspect of the business. They might like buying houses that need a lot of work. They might love planning out the design, managing the renovations, and creating cool and inspiring spaces. They may enjoy changing the look of an entire neighborhood and making a street where they grew up safer. Sometimes a new investor's focus is purely financial as they come to the realization that real estate is a tool to get them to a specific financial place or goal. There isn't a wrong answer to what is driving you, but understanding it and making it clear is critical.

Without understanding what it is you are pursuing with real estate—what parts of the business energize and excite you—it's easy to get distracted. Real estate offers many different opportunities and it can be hard to resist a venture and stay on course. Keeping that critical focus means every effort you make is directed at doing what you enjoy and creating the business and life you envisioned. If you don't keep that focus, you could easily look up, after years creating and running your business, and realize you are no closer to the goal than you were in the first place.

Early on when I started investing in real estate, I went after all kinds of different opportunities. I didn't stay focused on my vision of owning tens of millions in real estate, creating a financial legacy for my family, and giving away a million dollars a year. We invested in fix and flips. Holding rentals. Helping clients buy rentals. Owning and growing a property management company. Creating and designing multiple Airbnb properties. Buying land for new construction builds. Selling investment properties to clients for their own investments. We did have some success, and I made a great living, but I wasn't on target. My efforts weren't sufficiently focused on creating the experience in life I really wanted, or the specific business that would get me there.

In our own company, my partner and I finally understood that we needed to stay true to our vision of helping clients build wealth and freedom through real estate and to growing our personal real estate portfolio. Over the past six years, we've helped our clients add nearly fifty million dollars of real estate to their portfolios. And we are on our way to building and holding our own portfolio of that size over the next few years. If we had not paused to refocus our effort, our clients would not have grown their portfolios through our help. The mission of our company had to be clear and in alignment with the life and experience we wanted to create as owners and for our clients.

Take a moment to write down why you are getting into real estate. What experience, what feeling, what result are you looking for? Use this question to help create the big picture of what is driving and should be driving your business. Start to mentally lay the foundation of what kind of business you want to create—a business that will serve you, the team you work with, and your clients.

Defining Your Personal Achievement

What gives you a sense of achievement in real estate depends on you as an individual. You might feel that satisfaction when you help others in difficult situations with their homes. Or maybe designing and renovating a place someone will call home and grow their family gives you that feeling. It could come from creating financial independence for your own family or from building and growing an incredible company. Your why may be simply to own enough real estate to live and experience life without having to work a nine-to-five job. Whatever gives you pride and a sense of true success is the benchmark for achievement. It's all about fulfilling the why that you define.

The Definition of Financial Success

Without a clear definition of success, money can become an obsession and a hindrance that obscures your vision as you seek to live the life you really want. Money is simply a tool. You don't need a lot of money right now to start. You need a clear plan of action as you work to create the life you want and the determination to work every day toward it.

Early on, your first step toward financial success might simply be getting started with a few more books, going to the library for more study, or investing in a real estate course. Then, success might be taking steps toward owning your first BRRRR (Buy, Rehab, Rent, Refinance, Repeat) property, which may require that you do the majority of the renovation work yourself. After a number of properties are under your belt, you might define financial success with a dollar amount you are making per year as well as your net worth, which will increase with additions to your real estate portfolio every year.

As your portfolio grows, success will mean reviewing the cash you have on hand as you make more money and buy more real estate. Make sure that every month you hold some cash back for savings, taxes, issues, and opportunities that will come up in the future. The most successful investors I have known didn't necessarily have the most money or the biggest portfolio of investments in total, but they did have significant liquidity. Without having cash reserves that grow over time, something as simple as a larger repair on a rental house can put you massively in trouble because you didn't set aside cash for when you might need it.

When you are starting out, I'd encourage you to have three to six months of cash available to cover the mortgage of each of your properties, at least up to the first ten or fifteen you own. As your portfolio grows, as well as your cash reserves, you can then decide how much more you want to keep in savings and how much you put away each month. Every investor friend of mine has a slightly different plan, but every single one of them has a plan to ensure they have the cash to pay for repairs or cover months that don't produce the financial results they wanted—even with their best efforts. Rather than being surprised and unsure of what to do when an issue inevitably comes up, have your financial plan in place, know what it takes to cover your monthly expenses and build and sustain reserves that will keep you financially solid.

As your business expands, so will the sophistication of your financial plan. The better your plan, the more of your money you will keep through a clear tax, savings, and investment strategy. Create your financial plan from where you are today, and know that as you gain clarity on how to structure your income or the debts in your rentals, you can make adjustments. These recalculations are needed to grow, protect, and continue to stabilize your business and the life you've created.

Preparing to Succeed

Preparing for your dream to come to fruition might sound funny, but it is critically important right now as you see your business and your life coming together as you've laid it out. Nothing ever seems to happen exactly as we planned, but that doesn't mean we don't need to be prepared to be successful. You will create an incredible business while building your exceptional life, but it's time to imagine that life is here right now.

Starting today, consider yourself as a successful real estate investor. You create the budget for what your life will look like, making double what you make now . . . or triple . . . or even ten times as much. At one budget planning session of mine, I remember suddenly thinking, *what am I going to do with all this money I make every month?* It might sound crazy now, but if you put in the focused and sustained effort we've talked about, you will experience that same problem. Without having a plan now of what will happen when you do begin to experience a large cash flow, it will be easy to spend all the additional money you've made in ways that will not help you ultimately live the life you wanted to create.

More than a few times, I've made more money than I expected and screwed up by spending too much of it on things that didn't really matter. The time will come when you can spend a little money on something fun, amazing, or just because, and that expenditure will have little impact on your income or your financial stability. But start out by setting up the budget you will live on, the cash you will set aside as your investments grow, and the amount of money you will continue to invest in buying more real estate. Your amazing real estate business and your extraordinary life are on the other side of you creating, living out, and executing your plan.

Under Your Current Financial Hood

No matter what your current financial situation—massive credit card debt, student loans, or lots of cash but no plan—you can make the changes needed to be successful. Whatever you have done in the past can be fixed, setting you on course for what you really want your finances to be. But you must take stock of your current situation. Create a basic budget and calculate your net worth, and start tracking your financial health and growth. A budget and a net worth calculator are critical tools to understanding where you are financially, where the issues are that you need to address, and what steps to take next.

Creating a budget means you are telling every dollar that you make where it goes. You can be very detailed in examining your budget or create a few simple categories like housing, utilities, groceries, vehicles, taxes, entertainment, and investments. No matter what the categories are, track the amount of money that goes into each of those pots per month, and don't exceed what you have budgeted. You will have a sense of what your life really costs right now, but also more clarity about what you might want your budget to look like in the future as you are able to increase your income.

A net worth calculator adds up all of your assets while subtracting your debts. Your net worth is the difference between the two. If you are just out of school with a lot of student loan debt and a new car payment, it's likely that you might even have a negative net worth. We can't change the future without understanding where we are in the present, so don't get discouraged. Instead, use this process of learning as an important part of your financial education. It's always better to start creating what you really want financially and in life than to continue to live without a plan or not take any actions toward what you want.

Facing the Financial Facts

My buddy Dan and I were driving seventy miles an hour, trying to keep up with our friend who was leading the pack. We were on a road trip and would have several hours together in the car. We always had great talks and expected to cover a wide variety of entertaining topics. Dan had been excited about real estate for some time and steered the conversation to an idea he had for his budding real estate business.

"Nathan, I've got a real estate question for you if you don't mind."

"Of course, Dan. Let's do it, man. I love your enthusiasm for real estate and all the effort you put in."

Dan continued, his usual positive and gregarious personality shining through. "Yeah, man! So I saw this commercial building for sale not too far from my house. It looks like a pretty killer deal, so I was thinking about trying to buy it. There are a few other businesses in there, too, but I am not sure exactly what the situation is. I also think they would likely finance everything, but I haven't gotten into the specifics."

A little confused, I responded with a few clarifying questions. "That sounds like it could be an interesting opportunity. Honestly, I am not very familiar with investing in commercial buildings, but I'm sure if it's the right deal, I could help you find someone who would be of better help." Because we had talked mainly about investing in single-family houses in previous conversations, I was caught a little off guard by the opportunity he was pursuing. I asked, "Is commercial real estate what you are really excited about?"

He looked back over at me and said, "Not really, man. I am just excited to get started with something, and this looks like a really interesting opportunity. Real estate is awesome, and I really just want to get started as soon as possible!" he said with conviction.

I nodded, acknowledging our shared passion for real estate, and asked, "Did the bank say they could get the loan done for you? How much cash are you going to have to put down for all that? I just want to make sure you are prepared and ready for that deal if it's what you really want." I could see from his immediate concerned look there was more behind his questions than I knew.

I continued to ask him questions to try to understand his situation. How much did he have in savings? How much cash was he prepared to put down on the building? I also wanted to know about any investments he'd made and how they might affect his current net worth, debt, and savings in the short term. I needed a clear financial picture so I could point out any issues that might cause a problem as he sought to put this deal together. He was talking about his first investment in real estate, and I wanted to make sure he was set up to do it successfully.

As he began to answer the questions, I quickly realized we had missed a step or two in our previous conversations. Not only did Dan not have any money to put down on the building; he was sitting on a massive five-figure credit card debt that was causing serious financial hardship and frustration in his marriage. This was a situation he needed to address before making any large investments in real estate.

"Dan, listen, man. You probably aren't going to like this idea, but I don't think you should be investing in anything right now. If I were you, I'd put my entire focus on paying that credit card off. Take some extra odd jobs, make a little side cash, and put yourself in a more stable financial position. Otherwise, if you invest in real estate and anything goes wrong, you will have to rely on credit to bail you out. I've been there. I didn't start my investing business with the right financial footing, and I really paid for it when I ran out of cash early on."

We talked in depth about his financial struggles and what he wanted to see happen over the next few months. In true Dan fashion, after we talked through everything, he went home a few days later and put his plan in place. He and his wife had been paying barely more than the interest on their credit card debt each month, but they created a plan to pay down the card in less than eighteen months. Incredibly, after taking a hard look at their budget and seeing how fast they could pay it down by spending less, they had almost the entire thing paid off in less than nine months.

Real estate can change your life, and it will if you set up your business in a way that is sustainable and clear. But make sure you go into your new venture with your eyes open to your current situation, especially your finances. You will need the help of other investors, bankers, and private lenders along the way. They will all ask the same financial and business questions I asked Dan. You want to be financially prepared, understanding where you are and having a great plan in place, so you start from the strongest possible position to succeed.

Goal Setting Today with Your Future in Mind

To make the vision for your life and your business a reality, it has to be insanely clear and financial clarity is part of that. Not only should you understand the vision and the finances in detail, you need to be able to communicate them succinctly to your bankers, hard cash lenders, partners, investors, and real estate agents. You won't achieve the business you want all at once, it's going to happen in stages.

If owning one hundred rental properties is your goal, starting with the first few is a great first step. That doesn't mean you aren't going to hit the hundred you want, but you will have systems and processes to grow as you build your portfolio. Learn small, implement those lessons, and continue to grow and scale your business. Over and over, I've learned the hard way not to jump fully into a specific idea, process, or even new business idea without testing it first to make sure it creates the results I was expecting. Start small and test your assumptions and ideas. Learn from those tests and adjust until your investments are producing exactly what you want, and then scale them to produce the incredible end result you are after.

The business you are building isn't just about making money; it's building the foundation to live the most incredible life. Do a full financial review of where you are, your budget, your income, your net worth, and your current debts. Whatever you find, you can make the adjustments necessary and keep moving forward with positivity and by taking action. Finally, firmly hold the big-picture vision of what life will be like in mind, and start working back through the steps that will take you from where you are today to living your extraordinary life.

CHAPTER 10

CREATE A NO QUITTERS' PLAN

I have screwed up many times in my journey to create an incredible life and business. I've missed specific goals, failed to run the business the way I wanted it to run, and even failed to experience what I most hoped to in my business, family, and personal life. You are going to face your own challenges and difficulties. My failures helped me grow in ways I wouldn't have otherwise. I've learned lessons I wouldn't have without having endured the incredible and complex struggles of growing a business that serves me. The failures and lessons were necessary for me to develop into the leader and business owner I am now proud to be.

This year, our sixth year of business, we will sell tens of millions of dollars in real estate and will net seven figures. That sounds awesome, right? But I still face problems every day. I will never say that creating a real estate business or any business is easy, but creating a business that allows you to live the life you want is possible as long as you make what you want extremely clear—clear to you and to others. The clearer my partner and I have become in our vision of our extraordinary lives, the more we have been able to specifically align and build our company to that end. This isn't purely a business concept, but a concept that applies to every part of life. I'm sharing these lessons from my own experiences, so you can see how my partner and I have continually adjusted our business as it became clearer what we wanted it to do.

Over the past few years, Bridge Turnkey has not only bought, renovated, and sold tens of millions of dollars in real estate for our clients, but we've built our own portfolio of millions of dollars of rentals as well. As we came to understand what we wanted to hold long term, we sold off some properties, bought others, and began to build and scale our portfolio with new construction projects as well. Real estate that we own creates incredible passive income each month, and as we've scaled our portfolio, we've been able to take out substantial amounts of money tax-free by refinancing. Sometimes the most rewarding outcomes require time to come to fruition, but they are life-changing if you are willing to persevere through the challenges and execute the plan you have laid out. Real estate doesn't just serve you in creating income or building your wealth, but also in creating time for you to do and experience the things you want. I know I've said it before, but that *is* the basis of an extraordinary life.

Serving Others to Create an Extraordinary Life

One of the most deeply satisfying experiences of my life has been sorting through ideas and opportunities with my clients and students to help them identify and achieve their goals. I get to watch them transform a seed of an idea culled from some conversation, podcast story, or book into a dream and a plan. It's incredibly exciting seeing them succeed in creating the lives they want to live through investing in real estate and to share in their journeys. Our business team doesn't just put energy into finding the houses our clients want to buy or achieving the net worth they want to accrue, we work at understanding what life experience they want to create. Then we help them put in place the plan and strategies that will lead to that outcome.

Because I love helping, teaching, and inspiring investors, I decided to start a local real estate meetup in our market. We brought in some of the top real estate thought leaders and investors in the nation to speak and inspire, and worked hard to create an event that people would want to come back to. Our meetings quickly grew to hosting hundreds of budding and experienced local real estate investors who wanted to make connections. They got busy learning, growing, doing business, and finding their own path to the lives they wanted to live. It's one thing to possess the knowledge of how to invest in real estate and do it for yourself. For me, though, helping others do the same is even more rewarding. My understanding of what I can do through real estate not only dramatically changed my life, it is changing the lives of thousands of people who come to our events, read our posts, and share the knowledge. It's a great privilege and honor to make an impact on that scale.

My deep desire to help others create the lives they want is also why I decided to finally undertake writing this book. For more than two years, I have had this book concept sitting in my notes, staring back at me, harassing me constantly, asking me why I hadn't taken the action of writing it. But I knew I needed more of my own life experience to share why I am so passionate about real estate in a profound way. I have many friends and know many investors who make more money than I do, but I don't know many who live out their life, spend their time, in a way that gives them true joy. It is very important to me that you not only build a successful business that serves you, but you actually use your time and resulting financial resources to love the life you created. Not sometime in the future but right now.

Giving Away More Than Information and Inspiration

Since I was in high school, I've wanted an incredible life for myself, but I've also had a drive to help others. As a teen, I couldn't have imagined owning a real estate company, owning millions in properties, speaking on stages, or inspiring other investors. But I did imagine making enough money to live an awesome life and give to amazing causes that were making a difference.

Today, my goal is to create enough wealth in my personal life and business to give away one million dollars a year. I want to invest in organizations and people who have brilliant ideas about improving health, supporting the arts, and providing education for the kids in the community where I live. When choosing programs to support I thought about where my help would count the most. I am a big sports fan, but so often, sports programs receive a lot of attention, the biggest budgets, and the best gear and facilities. Because I spent time in high school and college singing in choirs and playing in orchestras all over the country, I got to see firsthand the disparity in funding for the arts compared to sports. I decided I would help change that.

My plan includes funding and helping now but is built to last for future generations as well. Even when I am no longer on the planet, the investment of my money and resources will still be making a lasting difference.

No matter what your vision of an incredible life looks like, don't miss the profound opportunity to give of yourself. Find an organization, a school, an idea, a city, or a country that you are both passionate about and want to help through your time and resources. You will experience greater fulfillment when you give and help others. Open your eyes to what calls to you, and be as inspired to do this as you are to build your business. Explore what gets you fired up, dream into it, and include it as a part of your big plan to change someone else's world. Helping to change someone else's life, is the epitome of living an extraordinary life.

Helping Others Create Their Own Extraordinary Lives

Just today, I was on a call with an investor friend of mine and, as we were talking, he said, "Nathan, I see all your social media posts of you out there traveling, exploring, hanging out with you son, living your life. You are a freedom and lifestyle guy now, you know? I love it!" He said my life was inspiring him to live his life doing the things that he really wants to do. I don't want to just inspire you, though. I want you to figure out how to live all out in the life you desire.

Here's the problem. You consistently spend time every week on things that you don't like doing. Think about it for a minute, and I bet you can come up with quite a list. Do you know what the solution is? Stop doing that stuff. If you don't like cleaning the house, hire a cleaner. Don't like dealing with the detailed tasks of accounting? Hire an administrator or accountant. We can get so wrapped up in what we feel we're supposed to do rather than what we want to do. Choose wisely.

By choosing what you want to spend your time doing, you will naturally work out a solution. Before, you might have thought, *I can't afford a cleaner.* But now, you ask yourself, *How can I not afford to get a cleaner? What would it take me in my business to earn enough money to cover the cost of reclaiming the time that I spend cleaning? I can figure this out because using my time doing something awesome is worth it.* Trading out time for things you don't like doing for things you do like may take time to figure out. Hold the vision of a life with more joy, work on creating that freedom in your life, and be inspired by others who have done the same.

You will start encountering more people who are on their own journey of creating their best life. There is a special positive power and energy you get from being around others who are both driven to pursue extraordinary lives and want you to be able to do the same. No matter where we are, how much money we make, or what our past experiences have been, we can connect and learn from each other. Inspire and be inspired. Learn and do life together. There isn't a more powerful human experience than learning, exploring, and experiencing life with like-minded people.

Creating Your No Quitters' Plan

It's time to determine the specific financial outcome you want to achieve. Consider where you want to live, what you drive, your budget for the things you love to do, and how you want your daily experience to play out in real life. Don't worry about what number you come up with; just be clear on why you came to that number and that it will give you the financial freedom you want.

Don't allow negative emotions around money to deter you from pursuing the amount of money you want to create and earn each month. Money is just money; it doesn't have emotions. It's a tool you will use to pay for the experiences you want. Use it to free up time spent on tasks you don't want to do. Hiring people to help you creates opportunities for them, and can help them to start to create the life they want.

You determine the income you want to make every month by creating a detailed budget of all your future life expenses. This includes regular monthly household expenses like the mortgage, utilities, vehicles, groceries, and insurance. It also includes travel, investing, and legal and accounting support. And put a substantial savings and investing plan in place. Everyone has a different amount of money they want to earn and life they want to live. Do not compare your desires to anyone else's. Put your complete focus and effort into your own plan, knowing that it's congruent with who you are. Now you have a financial goal. Reaching it will require you to be persistent and to work through challenges and problems that arise.

You are worthy of the incredible life you want.

Curating Your No Quitters' Team and Resources for Success

Once you have laid out the future budget and have clarity regarding the big picture you want to create, it's time to put together the rest of your team. Remember other people are key to accomplishing what you want. You can't go it alone and experience real success.

For your business team, you will need an attorney you trust and communicate well with who understands your goals. Also, a title company or closing attorney who is responsive, communicative, and has a history of working with investors. Find a CPA who doesn't just file taxes but understands real estate. They will be instrumental in creatively planning around what you buy, what you sell, and how to make the best financial decisions for the long term.

Start thinking of who else you need in your life to help you build your real estate business. If you don't like details, you will want to think about hiring an administrative person who can help manage details. A project manager as you scale projects. And someone who's brilliant with sales if you decide to list or sell the properties you renovate or build. Every business is a little different but has the same basic components of operations: sales and marketing, administration, and finance. Don't let any of these areas surprise you; prepare for them now. As things come up you don't understand, reach out to your team and work through decisions that must be made. If someone else needs to be hired or brought in to solve problems none of you know how to solve, do that. Success isn't rooted in you having all the answers. It comes when you surround yourself with the most incredibly talented people you can find who are also connected to the vision you have laid out.

It is imperative you are constantly learning and growing. I always tell my team I expect to set the bar of always getting better and I have the same expectation of them. There are numerous books on real estate, business development, and personal development. There are podcasts on big-picture topics like what to invest in that drill down to detailed planning, strategy, and problem-solving. Connecting at local meetups or national real estate events is fabulous for learning, sharing, and finding more clarity and direction in what you are working on. Investing in coaching and mastermind groups has brought us lifelong friends and colleagues, and exponentially increased our abilities and understanding, which we apply in many areas of our lives. Learning and growing never ends.

Prepare for Your Plan to *Work*

When I start working with my students and clients, I challenge them to focus not on what won't work or on the fears they need to overcome but on the incredible outcome they want. I challenge you right now to do the same. Write down the fears that are dragging you down, and work on adding contingencies to your plan to help you overcome them. Then, come back to the vision you have laid out, and feel the intensity of that experience in your body, your heart, and your mind. We aren't preparing for failure, we are preparing for whatever it takes to create success. Tell yourself every day, "I will be successful."

Prepare yourself now for what it will feel like when you've succeeded in creating your extraordinary life. The work that it will take. The journeys and experiences you will have because of the work, effort, and determination that you have put in to get here. Breathe. Hold your incredible life in your mind, and feel both the power and the gratitude you have for this accomplishment. Your life will never be the same because you have manifested the life you want to live.

You may encounter people who deluge you with negative or ignorant comments about your ideas, your goals, and your vision. Their opinion of your ideas and what you are creating doesn't matter. Your goals and your feelings are yours to care for and make real. It is not for anyone else to tell you what is right or to direct you without your request for help. I want you to realize that in every moment, you can experience the joy of the life you have right now. You aren't creating a life for some point in the future; you are creating it to live and enjoy from today to forever.

Creating an Incredible Daily Experience

Your life and the time you spend intentionally living it is your responsibility. Take out your journal or your notebook and write out the fun activities, learning, and hobbies that you want to spend your time on every week. If you find this difficult, you are not alone. I find that about half of my students have an easy time with this, and the other half struggle to picture what they would do. Whatever comes to mind and whatever chances to come up are okay.

You will have new incredible opportunities arise all the time, and now you will have created the time and financial freedom to experience them. I just spent an entire week this month with a massive sixty-pound flying contraption strapped on my back. I was learning to fly a powered paraglider over the vast salt flats of Utah. This opportunity wasn't on my radar until one of our business coaches suggested it. It sounded intriguing and I was able to say *yes*. This was possible because I intentionally created both the wealth and the time in my life to have these experiences. You, too, can create that space in your life.

I ask my students to print out a blank calendar and fill in their perfect day. You know my day starts with meditation, journaling, and then some sort of short full-body workout to get my mind and body going for the day. After a short workout, I block time to enjoy coloring with my daughter or listening to the current audio book I am reading. Next, I dig into some important work for a few hours before heading to the MMA gym for a midday training session. In the early afternoon, I take an important call with a friend or explore a new and interesting business opportunity. After hitting some golf balls at the driving range near my house, I head home to toss steaks on the grill and pour a fantastic bourbon in my glass.

Anyone who knows me will tell you the day I just laid out is actually how I live my life. It's not a fantasy; it's the life I planned out and executed piece by piece, so I could experience the life I want every day. I am giving you permission to do the same with your life—live it however you want.

If you are still struggling to come up with how you would spend your time, don't stress. Instead, block out an hour on your calendar every day to read interesting books, watch fascinating YouTube videos, or explore concepts or experiences that come up. Enjoy the process of discovering what you want. Write down some ideas for what looks exciting, inspiring, fun, or rewarding and add them to your calendar and try them out. Take a lesson, attend a class, or test your fitness. When something new comes up, you will have created the conditions to be able to go after it. Find out what you love and want to experience more.

Lastly, stop telling yourself you don't have the time to go to the gym, drive golf balls, or whatever it is that you want to do. This is a lie you are telling yourself. You just haven't made your new life important enough. Even if you have been working your current job for some time and haven't yet created a real estate business that produces a totally different financial and time capacity for you, I am telling you to block out time every day for *you*. Building your business and your new experience, creating your vision, and living your life is your new reality. You must start it today, not wait for some distant time in the future.

Prepare Your Financial Plan Today for Tomorrow

Just as you have created your vision, the picture of your life, and the experiences you want to enjoy, you need to prepare for financial success. Making a lot more money will give you new opportunities to invest it, grow it, and use it for marvelous things. Think of the financial advisor you will need to have in your circle who both understands real estate and anything else—stocks, metals, crypto, etc.—that you might be interested in investing in. You are preparing for having far more money than you need to live your life and what you will do with it.

You will also seek out new friends and colleagues who are also trying to answer these same questions. You'll discuss money, investments, and opportunities with financially successful entrepreneurs who are living their lives the way they want to. The team around you will grow, as you add a CFO to your staff or an attorney or mentor who can guide you. As you are more and more successful in each area of your life, you will continue to attract more and more people who are on the same journey.

With the increase in your income, you also now have the newfound freedom to spend money on things that just make you happy. I have found several things that spark joy for me. Training with a professional MMA coach each week. Having clubs fitted and taking lessons with a golf coach. Heading into the mountains for days of adventure with the best gear money can buy. Taking my son on memorable guided fishing adventures all over the country. What does your incredible life look like? Your imagination and desire for experience is the only limiting factor.

What Do You Do When You Feel Defeated?

No matter how great your plan is or how hard you work, you will experience difficulties and challenges. But you can be prepared for them. If low cash flow could be a problem, make sure you set aside money to have financial reserves as you grow. If funding might fall through or be difficult to secure, establish more great relationships with your banking and lending partners. These could make the difference when you need to borrow in a tight spot. Financial stress can be oppressive if you haven't taken the time to create contingency plans for what you need to do when issues come up.

Learning from your problems is also key. Dealing with renters in your properties or contractors who are renovating a property can be a major hassle. My team has spent the last six years buying and renovating hundreds of homes, and we still have regular challenges every week that we have to overcome. Embrace every one of these experiences as opportunities to learn and plan better, and integrate the learning into your processes so today's problems don't also become tomorrow's.

Instead of holding an issue inside as you try to solve it yourself, remember that you built a team, hired coaches, and found mentors for a reason. I reach out to my friends, coaches, and colleagues regularly when issues come up, and they reach out to me for the same. Sometimes a problem is so close to us that we have a hard time mentally and emotionally working through it without the help of an outside perspective—someone who can be objective. You aren't weak or incapable of solving the problem; you are strong and have the courage to seek out the best advice and solve the problem with the best possible outcome.

In moments when you feel like your vision will never come together, take the time to slow down and come back to what is really important. Understand and recognize the negative emotion as it comes up, and name it. Dig into what is really causing the anxiety and write it down. For example, you might buy a house and negotiate a timeline and budget for renovations with a contractor only to discover after demolition work there were bigger issues that will cost more time and money to repair. You feel frustrated and discouraged, but the real fear is that your exceptional life is slipping out of reach. Take the time to breathe and meditate, go for a walk, and let those overwhelming thoughts run through your brain. Then, let them go. When you return to the problem you will have perspective and see it is just an obstacle you will work around to get to your goal.

Practice moving into a powerful and positive state before making decisions. I use a specific podcast or style of music to help me do that. Once you have identified the emotion you are feeling and the problem that needs to be solved, then you can devise a clear strategy to solve it. Remind yourself you are not only capable of solving the problem but will make the best possible decision with the information you have. Going through bankruptcy reminded me often that a difficult experience in the moment is not the final outcome. You can work through whatever obstacle, big or small, that is in front of you.

Regularly come back to your journal and reread the vision you have laid out for your life, your business, and the experience you want to create. Check the decisions and opportunities you are pursuing to make sure they are in alignment. I've worked for months on projects only to realize they didn't fit our business or my life. If a project didn't fit, no matter how much I liked it at the time, I immediately stopped moving forward with it. I've had to make these hard decisions over the years with stopping business projects or letting people go on our team, and they can be excruciating. Make the tough calls, get things back in alignment and get back after it.

The more you focus on what you want life to look like, the easier it is to say no to opportunities or decisions that don't fit. When you know what you want to experience in your personal life, in your business, and in time with your family and friends, you'll make decisions with confidence in alignment with the life you are creating.

The more complete your vision of life, the more effectively and rapidly you will build what you want. Then, not only do you live out the life you want, but you'll help inspire others to do the same. Even when problems and challenges arise, you are prepared to overcome them with your plan, the team around you, and your No Quitters' attitude. You laid out what you wanted life to look like and now you get to experience it.

CHAPTER 11

EXECUTE THE PLAN

Visualize yourself doing something that makes you feel incredibly successful, deeply fulfilled, and joyful. Close your eyes. Picture the experience in full detail and feel the power of the scene you created. Don't rush through this; spend a few minutes in the vivid virtual reality of your imagination and enjoy it

The practice of visualization develops a strong mental muscle you can use to put yourself into a positive mindset whenever you want. Not only does visualization make you feel amazing, it allows you to experience every piece of your extraordinary life even before you bring it into being. You can use visualization to test whether something you think you want in your life will actually produce the feeling and experience you want. Anytime you have a new idea or opportunity, you can play it in your mind before you take action.

For years, I dreamt of the home that I wanted to live in in great detail. I constantly visualized driving down the long and winding driveway and catching sight of the columns that added height and stateliness to a house perfectly sited on well-manicured acres. Inside the house was a beautiful open kitchen for entertaining and enjoying my family. Outside was a yard large enough to host beautiful summer evenings with large bonfires and a deck large enough for grilling amazing meals while enjoying awesome conversations.

This is the exact house I call home today. Right now, I'm sitting here at my custom-built picnic table on the huge deck in the back of the house while I sip a great glass of wine and write this book. The trees cover nearly the full eleven acres of the property surrounding the house, and deer, turkeys, and foxes are regular guests at our place. From the moment I drove down the driveway and walked through the front door, I knew this home would be mine. It was just one massive problem to figure out how I was going to buy it.

The problem was the day I walked the house I didn't actually have the cash to buy it. Not even close. However, after spending a few minutes in the house, I knew no matter what I had to figure out how to purchase it. I ran through every possible way I could put a deal together: seller financing, local banks that might work with me, and asking friends to help in the short-term by lending the down payment to make it happen. This house was going to be mine, and nothing was going to stop me from buying it.

That night, after driving home deep in thought, I walked across the street to my neighbor and literally sold my house to him after a brief conversation. Then I selected the lowest-performing rentals my wife and I owned and sold off six of them within the next seven days. I combined my clarity about the home I wanted, the real estate business and personal assets I owned, and the sales and marketing skills I had learned along the way to solve the problem in front of me.

We closed on our new home just forty or so days later, having put together almost six figures in cash from the sales of the rentals. After selling our previous residence to the neighbor, we completed the financing with the bank to purchase the house. Don't tell yourself you can't figure out the problem in front of you no matter how difficult or complex it might be. Decide now the life you want to live is worth achieving whatever problems you must solve to get there.

Visualize Living Your Incredible Life

Now it's your turn to paint the picture of the beautiful place you want to call home. Visualize it in detail. See the front door as you open it and walk into the living space. What kinds of experiences do you have there? Are you hosting small dinner parties with friends? Or showing one or two people in your life your wine cellar, or your killer workout space, or the library room that inspires you every time you enter? Maybe your favorite feature is the kidney-shaped pool perfectly set in the backyard you see from the large picture windows in the chef's kitchen. Or the patio beside it where your family relaxes together and makes many wonderful memories. Success doesn't mean you need to own a massive house. Maybe your dream home is a small cabin outfitted perfectly for you to live simply. Success means you can decide what your life, your home, and your experience will be as you create every part of it the way you want.

Since high school, I've dreamt of owning my favorite car of all time, the Porsche 911. You can't convince me it's not the sexiest car ever created. I knew I had to have one and visualized exactly how it would feel to sit behind the wheel. Early on, I set one rule for myself: I wouldn't go test-drive one until I could afford to buy one. After imagining driving that car for more than a decade, my first test-drive delivered an exhilarating experience; the car was everything I had hoped. Even at over six feet tall, I could fit into it. Within just a few weeks of test-driving one, I found the perfect seven-speed, low-mileage Porsche 911 three states away. I negotiated the deal over the phone and bought the car sight unseen. I didn't *need* a sports car, but it brings me joy every time I sit in the cockpit, turn the key, and take it for a drive. My car was part of what I wanted and visualized as my extraordinary life. I've created a business and a lifestyle that allowed me to afford it, and you can do the same.

You can also visualize how you want your relationships to feel. Imagine having amazing family time together. You are fully present and supportive of your kids at their soccer games or listening with full concentration as they play in band performances. Imagine creative and fun date nights with your spouse. Where do you like to go together? Do you like exploring new things as a couple, like taking a cooking class or learning to dance? Now imagine time with your friends. Are you sipping afternoon cocktails together or running a marathon side by side? Do you imagine fun vacations with family and friends you adore? You will have the time and money to travel and do the things you want. Your extraordinary life is heightened by all the love and connections you make in each interaction and experience. You built your life so that every day you could spend your time with the people you care about doing what you want. Put the vision of that experience firmly in place.

Some of my most amazing family, friend, and personal moments have happened because I had the financial resources and time to say yes when opportunities came up. A guided fishing trip with my son on the Madison River in Montana. Last-minute cross-country flights to San Diego and Tampa. Strapping a motor on my back and learning how to launch myself into the air when I tried power paragliding. Spending an entertaining week with friends at a hillside mansion in Mexico that overlooked the ocean, with meals prepared by a private chef. Life changed completely when I could simply consider an opportunity and decide if I or my family wanted to do it instead of wondering if we had the time or could afford it.

You get to create your life in whatever way you want. Playing at your favorite park with your kids. Savor an aged filet mignon and a bottle of Paso Robles red at your favorite local steakhouse. You pursue activities and hobbies because they are of interest to you. The most amazing part of all of this is that you can start living this way right now. Seek out what it is that you want in your life, and begin planning, dreaming, and living that way. You might not get to play golf every day, but you could budget and create time to play once or twice a month. Find the best restaurants in town and put away a fund to occasionally go out to dinner. Yes, you can start living your incredible life right now. Your extraordinary life is not meant to be lived sometime in the future. It is meant to be lived starting today.

Use Your Incredible Life to Inspire, Help, and Connect with Other Amazing People

Creating and experiencing the life you want doesn't just affect you. Your new life will become an inspiration to the people around you. Many of your friends, connections at church or community groups, social networks, and work colleagues will become curious and somewhat perplexed by how you accomplished what you have. Some will want to understand how you did it and how they can create a fabulous life, too. Others may be envious and make comments on how lucky you are or how they wish they could have a life like yours. No matter how hard it might be, don't live one moment with any negativity. Your extraordinary life is built for the purpose of living it regardless of what anyone else thinks.

It's interesting that as I started to manifest my vision, other people reached out to me who wanted profound joy in their life. You will become part of a community of like-minded people who want to have the same incredible experience of life that you do. Imagine the wild adventures and beautiful moments you will have with people in your life who you deeply care for. I've built many new relationships based on the shared values of love, connection, and living life with purpose. These wonderful new friends all want to live to their full potential, and my life is better for having them in it. They have opened many new business opportunities for me as well as amazing personal experiences.

While you are on all your incredible adventures, connecting with new and old friends, you will find your conversations dramatically change. Instead of talking about how to make a few extra dollars or how much everyone hates their jobs, your new group will be focused on how to further improve their businesses, family, or personal lives. I've found myself learning new business tactics and new ways to approach personal difficulties from new friends who have met and overcome the same problems. I've completely changed my life by filling it with people I love to be around who inspire each other and constantly seek to live satisfying and meaningful lives.

Some People Won't Be a Fit for Your Incredible Life

Part of the No Quitters' experience is recognizing the life you are creating is not for everyone. Some people don't have the patience, the self-belief, or the drive to do the work that is required to change their path. No matter how unfulfilled, broken, or lacking in financial resources, they won't be interested in making changes even if they understand that it could lead them to an incredible life. These naysayers will hold onto a belief that creating an incredible life is impossible for them—impossible because of their status in society, their current financial situation, or their level of education. These beliefs are all invalid, but there will be nothing you can do to change their minds or the direction of their lives.

Old friends and family members may find it the hardest to understand the changes you are making and the desires you have. They may make resentful comments to you, wondering why your life is expanding in joy and theirs is not. Part of learning and growing in life involves appreciating people for who they are while also understanding you don't have any responsibility for their lives or decisions. This includes your brothers, sisters, parents, spouse, children, and closest friends. These may be people you hold in high regard or have looked up to for a long time, but ultimately, you have to create the experience of life that you want, and they are responsible for creating their own.

One of the most important changes I made in my life was to stop being around negative people. These are people who aren't trying to build their lives, themselves, or others up, who aren't open to learning and growing, and who blame others for where they are now instead of putting in the effort to change. Anytime I was around someone like this, I felt trapped, and I wanted to immediately get away from their negative words and energy. When I finally committed to removing negative people from my life, it was one of the most impactful and important decisions I've ever made. I have chosen to make every interaction, every relationship, one of love, joy, fun, and positivity that further creates the life I want to live.

Sometimes, removing these people from your life is as easy as not going to certain parties, events they are involved in, or a local restaurant or bar where you might see them. Other times, it's harder. I have even initiated a direct conversation with someone to end a negative relationship. I wish the person well but let them know I won't be connecting in the same way anymore. I wish them the best success in finding joy and happiness in their lives, and then I move on. I've never once regretted no longer associating with people who weren't a fit, but I've always suffered when I didn't make the decision to move on once I realized there was an issue.

Other incongruities in your relationships might include people's personal habits like excessive drinking, not taking care of themselves physically, or who they hang out with. To be clear, I try consciously to not make judgments about other people and how they are living their lives. Choose the people you spend your life with thoughtfully. Allow them to be an inspiration for the incredible life you are living.

Live Your Life with Intention

I've spent a lot of time on how you can visualize the life you want. Imagining what it looks like. How you will spend your time. How you will build an incredible business that serves you. What it will feel like to create and live your life in a way that will inspire and help other people transform their lives. It's time now to take all those pieces of your vision, put them together, and begin executing your plan.

Understand the vision and purpose of what you are creating and how it will change your life forever. Write about it in your journal and about how your business is growing into one that serves you and your why. Once that is clear to you, you are ready to share it. In every conversation with every person whether they are new to your life or a longstanding part of it, share what you are up to. Unabashedly, tell the world what you are doing and planning. Pour the excitement you have for what you are creating into everything you do.

By sharing the vision you have created for your life, you get to see how it feels as you tell the world. You are trying on this new life you are creating, like going to a clothing store and trying on a new pair of pants. You need to make sure you like the material, the color, and the fit. Test out this incredible new you to make sure it feels authentic and congruent with what you really want. If it feels amazing to share every idea, if it fires you up, you are on the right path. If you feel some tension about or resistance to sharing what you're vision is, that doesn't mean you have failed or that you can't create what you want. It only means you have more work to do in either clarifying what you want or the direction you want to go in some part of your business, family, or personal life.

Align all of your actions and your thoughts with the outcome you are working toward. Make sure every day you come back to your why, your purpose that extends beyond you as an individual. Visualize what you are creating in great detail as if it has already come to be. Hold the incredible impact of what you are creating in your mind as you solve every problem that comes up. Make the best decisions possible, and execute your game plan toward the end result you want. The only person responsible for creating your incredible life is you.

Know that every decision and plan you make in business, in your family life, and your personal life, won't always go the way you expect it to. Plan on it. Part of building the life you want means you will face some challenges that will help reinforce what you don't want. Often the experiences that are hardest are also the most powerful and impactful long term. Don't be afraid of failing. Be open to the experience of learning, and use the lessons you've learned to improve your plan and pursue the ultimate outcome of building the life you want.

How Goals and Your Definition of Your Extraordinary Life Change over Time

The goals you set today will almost certainly change over time. Whether it's the amount of money you want to make or the time and energy you want to spend working, what is important to you will change. Embrace knowing change is part of the journey of creating your incredible life. These changes might include where you live, the work that you find satisfying, or how you want to spend your time. Early in my career, I loved working insanely long days, constantly on the go. Today, I find enormous satisfaction in working much less but with more focused time building cool new partnerships and putting together big deals that have a major impact.

I also love taking golf lessons, learning how to drive the ball better, and be more consistent with my swing. I'm not even close to accomplishing that yet, but I love the learning and challenge of this new sport I can play until they have to haul me off the golf course. Just a few years ago, golf wasn't even on my radar. Because I've created the time and financial freedom in my life, I can now pursue whatever it is that sounds interesting and give all the time and attention to it that I want.

For me, part of the satisfaction of playing golf or pursuing anything worthy in life is the learning that's required. I don't care what you choose to get into, but go all in. Study it. Be passionate and love the time you are spending on your hobby or business venture. Hire a great coach. Lay out the personal goals you have for that hobby, and go after them. If it's golf, hit balls two or three times a week. I took twenty lessons in my first year of playing so that I could be proficient enough to say yes to invitations to play with friends and new business connections. Ultimately, I broke 100 for a round of golf in that first year. Life is more fun when you challenge yourself and surround yourself with people who will push you while you're having great fun doing whatever it is you want.

Every day, it's your responsibility to connect back to the life you want to create for yourself and assess where you are in relation to it. Plan regular gut checks to see if what you want is in alignment with what you are actually working on. Make the adjustments necessary to ensure that the work you are doing and the outcome you want are perfectly lined up. Sometimes you will realize that they aren't, and that's okay. Once you realize it, you have all the tools you need to reconnect with your why—the vision you want to hold—and tweak or change your course. Refine what you need to, and hold steady with what is working and what you love. The life you live is the expression and creation of whatever it is that you want it to be.

No matter what, believe in your heart and your mind that you can and will create the incredible life you want. I repeat: You can create it and you will. No problem will be too difficult to overcome. Challenges will be moments for learning and growing. Experiences you don't like will help guide you to more that you will love. The path you take might not look exactly like what you expected in the beginning, but that was only an expectation. You have the power right now to learn whatever you need to learn, make whatever decision is in front of you, and build the most extraordinary life you can imagine.

As you prepare for success, allow yourself to dream of the home you want to live in, the car you want to drive, and how it will feel to accomplish everything you've laid out. Enjoy the moments you will have with the people in your life who you love. As you connect and meet new people, your life will be a deep inspiration for others to create their own incredible lives. Build and surround yourself with a group of people who share the values, beliefs, and passions for life that you do. Not everyone in your life today will likely fit in that group, and that's okay. From today forward, you will spend your time visualizing, executing, and building your life exactly the way you want it to be. Enjoy the process, and know that you will be successful. The only limiting factors are the vision you create and your determination to accomplish what you want. Have patience as it comes together and persevere to stay the course you've laid out.

CHAPTER 12

THE NO QUITTERS' PATH: SUCCESS IN THE EXECUTION

On the journey to my exceptional life, I have established routine practices that have kept me on the path to my vision. Some of these started small and were expanded. Others I began as experiments and refined. But all of the practices I share in this chapter have had enormous impact on my ability to execute my plan and reach goals.

Start every day by defining what success looks like for you. Spell out what is most important and what you specifically need to do to accomplish your goals and the feeling you want to experience. Establish a clear intention. The more you do this, the more easily you can align how you are spending your time with the end result you really want. This practice will help tremendously whether you are starting your business, going through difficult times, or refining what is important.

Bring positive energy and a belief in yourself to every moment. At the beginning of a new project, an incredible opportunity, or a difficult challenge, remember you can create whatever life and experience you want. You can build an amazing business you are proud of that produces however much money you want to make. You will be able to buy the spectacular house you always dreamt of in your favorite dream location. Your success has no limits if you have a clear vision and take the actions you need to achieve it.

Appreciate the hard work ahead of you. Remember your life up to now has made you the person you are. Every lesson, hardship, and experience contributes. No matter where you are on the path to building your exceptional life, don't be frustrated with your current situation. Name where you are, and where you want to go, and then put all your focus on what you want your life to look like. Make it your reality.

Build a Strong Mental Game

Establishing the daily practice of meditation is a first step toward achieving and maintaining an incredibly positive mindset. Meditation is about listening quietly to what's happening in your mind and making space to process all the thoughts you have about the work you are doing and life experiences you're are having. Through this practice, you will connect your conscious and subconscious thoughts and make them congruent with the actions you are taking. You will better understand the root cause of whatever negative feelings you experience so that you can effectively work through the problem or situation. I've also found that when I meditate the manic thoughts that are constantly pinging in my head slow down, making me calmer and more able to focus on what is in front of me.

I won't describe any meditation techniques here. Try out a few different meditation apps, lessons, or books to see what works best for you. Give yourself grace as you learn and experience this new practice. I still struggle at times to just be present and in the moment even for ten minutes of meditation. But the more you meditate, the more comfortable you will become, and the more you will experience its benefits. Remember that this practice isn't a win-or-lose challenge; it is meant to bring awareness of your thoughts. This mental work will help you be appreciative of and present in every moment going forward.

Our thoughts are powerful and often drive what we do even without our realizing it. Mental work every day helps us to stop and recognize what thoughts are coming up and then what those thoughts are telling us. Ask yourself: *Are the things that I am thinking about really going to produce the incredible life and experience I want?* The more consistent I am with my meditation practice, the more easily I am able to understand what I am feeling and the thoughts I am having, and then I can take action in the most positive and effective way.

Since I started meditating, I've been able to make better decisions, I am also a genuinely happier and more patient person. When an anxious feeling comes on, instead of operating from that negative place, I now have a tool to help me reflect on why I am feeling that way. I name the issue, and dig into what is causing that feeling. I address whatever the issue is that is coming up directly, even if my action is as simple as naming what is uncomfortable. You will be amazed by how much better you feel as you move back into a powerful mindset just by naming whatever issue is arising.

Imagine making every decision for your business, your family, and your personal life from a positive and powerful mental state. Couple this positive state with a consistent belief in the plan you have created, and operate from that place. All of your thoughts are in alignment as you tell yourself that not only is the plan an awesome one, but nothing is stopping you from accomplishing your mission and realizing the vision for your life. You will be successful.

Get Physical Daily

Just like your mental practice of meditation, putting your body through physical activity every day is critical to your success. Working out daily is part of staying healthy mentally and physically. Exercise helps you destress and reset your mental state. Don't sit in negative emotions or feelings for long; they are a reminder that you need to address a problem, but you need to be in the right emotional state to do that. The negative emotions you experience aren't there to help you long term, but they are very helpful in the short term to recognize where you need to put your focus and effort. When I feel overwhelming negative emotions, I know that I must get up, get moving, and change the emotional state I am in.

One of the most powerful tools I use all the time to move past a problem, get creative, or settle down mentally is to simply get up and move. I go outside for a walk as I work through a problem. I feel the weight of my golf club hitting the ball as I spend an hour at the driving range processing a new opportunity. When I'm training in the MMA gym, I'm so locked into the physical nature of the workout that I can't focus on anything but the person in front of me. Most of the time, I realize after the workout that I've forgotten altogether what was stressing me in the first place and can now approach the problem in a much clearer and more positive frame of mind.

It doesn't matter what physical activity you choose, just get your body moving. Run, walk, lift weights, do some push-ups and squats in your office, play your favorite sport. Exercise is not only good for your health but will give you time and space to decompress and be ready for the rest of your day. Your incredible life requires that you are able to live it, doing whatever you truly want to do. An incredible life does not require working round the clock to the point that you neglect your health and wellbeing. Eat nutritious food. Drink lots of water. Open a great bottle of red wine. Get your exercise in. Your physical practice is as important as your mental practice in building the life you want to have.

Write Everything Down

Once I started my daily journal practice, my ability to go from seeing an opportunity to accomplishing it increased dramatically. I was more focused on the goals I set and the action I took to accomplish them. Every time I opened my journal, I saw everything I was working on written out, staring me in the face. I wasn't only clearer on what the big goals were, but the actions that I needed to take and the incredible impact they would have on my life.

Journaling is a way to get the thoughts, ideas, and plans you have inside your head out where you can better examine and evaluate them. Notice how ideas feel as you write them down. Read them out loud. Bringing thoughts and ideas into the world is not a small thing. I found that once I started to journal, my ability to take ideas to fruition massively improved. I wasn't just forming an idea of how to create something I wanted. Journaling made me write down what the idea was, why it was important, and then what the concrete steps were that I needed to take to accomplish them.

From a big-picture perspective, you'll remember I begin every quarter with the three major outcomes I want to achieve. I set one business goal, one family goal, and one personal goal. These range from major revenue or staffing goals for the company to calendaring and spending weekly dates with my kids. Write out what it will mean for you to establish and honor these commitments in your life, how it will feel, and why they are important. Spell out how your focus will lead to the results you achieve.

My daily journaling practice started with writing down three things I was grateful for each day, which is still part of my morning routine. It might sound easy, but some days just don't seem to start the way you want them to. You face problems that you didn't anticipate. No matter how frustrating or difficult the problems are in your life, there are always things you have to be grateful for. Starting with gratitude helps you shift back into thinking positively and coming at whatever challenge is ahead of you with positive mental energy.

In addition to writing down quarterly goals and three things that I am grateful for each day, I like to write down what is working really well for me that week. Ask yourself, *In what areas of my life have I been creating what I really want?* Write your answer down and appreciate the effort that you have been making. I also write about areas of my life where I didn't put enough focus and why it's important to give them due attention. Then I immediately create the action items I need to work on and put them on my calendar for the week. I reserve the time I planned and use it to do the work to accomplish whatever I committed to doing. This practice ensures you put your attention and effort on what you want to accomplish and creates momentum toward your exceptional life.

Lastly, I do a final review of the actions I've laid out for the week and ensure they are congruent with the quarterly goals I set. I then look through the calendar for the week and schedule the time I will be spending to produce the goals I laid out for myself. I hold myself accountable for doing the work I need to do to build the life I want. You can too.

Define What Winning Looks Like

Spell out in detail in your journal what winning your week looks like. Is it reaching out and connecting with sellers to find more houses you want to buy? Or connecting with your mentor or coach to sort out whether something new might be getting in the way of accomplishing your next goal? Or spending more time with your spouse? After defining what winning the week looks like, put in the effort to win. You will not build your extraordinary life without putting in the work it takes to create it.

By laying out your goals, you have a clear objective to accomplish. I usually like to have two or three big things that are mission-critical each week. This allows me to stay highly focused on what's really important. It also keeps me from adding more tasks, meetings, or other agenda items during the week. Stay focused and dialed in to solve the biggest issues and opportunities that will create the most impact for the week, the month, and the quarter so that you can achieve the goals you've set for yourself.

At the end of the week, I review the goals I set that week and the work I did, to confirm that I completed everything I set out to accomplish. In my journal, I cross out each item I completed. I add the date of completion above the item so there is no question that I did the task. Then I reread the goals I set for the quarter and think about the next few steps I need to focus on to accomplish my goals.

No one is going to hold you accountable for accomplishing your goals but you. You define what winning looks like. You will produce whatever results you create with your focus, your time, and your energy. Thoughtfully and wisely choose your goals each week, month, and quarter. Make every effort in your life congruent with visualizing, creating, building, and executing your most extraordinary life.

To help motivate me and to celebrate steady effort, I offer myself incentives. When the quarter is over, I go back and read the goals I laid out and why they were important. I confirm I accomplished what I set out to achieve. At the beginning of each quarter, I always pick a reward for accomplishing the goals I set for that quarter. Sometimes it's a family trip or something I really want to try for a hobby. The actual reward doesn't matter as much as the feeling you will have after setting a goal, crushing it, and enjoying your success.

Review Your Business Goals and Execute

In our business, the leadership team meets every quarter to review our performance in relation to the goals we set for the year. We also identify problem areas in the business, challenges in our team's performance, and other obstacles that could stand in the way of accomplishing our mission. In open and honest dialogue, we hash out whatever is happening, good or bad.

We review in detail the company's financial performance down to how much profit we made each month and for the quarter. Not only do we share that information, but we give bonuses—a portion of the profit that quarter goes to the entire team. We want every member to be connected to our goals and to understand and accomplish the parts and pieces that are their responsibility. The financial incentives are intentionally in alignment with each person working together as part of the team to execute the goals we've laid out.

You may not have a leadership team or even any employees at this point in your business. But wherever you are on your journey is okay. You might be at the point of clarifying your vision and establishing next steps that will lead to what you really want. But don't assess whether you are successful in accomplishing your goals compared to my business or anyone else's. Base your assessment on whether the goals *you* set were accomplished, moving you closer to what you want.

Schedule your own quarterly reviews no matter how big or small your business is. Bring in your mentor or friends who are in similar places with their businesses so you can help hold each other accountable. It might cost you something to have a professional mentor or business coach be a part of your meetings, but it's worth it. We pay to get outside perspective and the biggest and best real estate investors I know all use professional help in their business planning. They are successful because they surround themselves with people who keep them focused on their mission, recognize issues, solve them, and help them plan for future actions that lead to accomplishing goals.

The focus and accountability from our quarterly meetings have transformed our business. The meetings have brought us back on track when we've made decisions or taken actions that weren't really helping us accomplish the big-picture goals we had laid out for ourselves. They have changed my business and helped me create the life I wanted to live.

Tools for Running Your Business Effectively

Building a business is not easy, but there are many people who have gone before you who have done it and been incredibly successful. The first book I always suggest for new business owners is *The E-Myth* by Michael Gerber. It's an awesome book that not only deals with the positive dreams you have about becoming an entrepreneur, but the lessons and challenges that you will encounter along the way. Once you've finished *The No Quitters' Guide* and laid out your big vision for what you want life to look like, *The E-Myth* would be an awesome next book to read as you think about what your business looks like, how you want your company to operate, and what you will need to think about and solve as you build it.

My partner and I were also introduced to *Traction* by Gino Wickman at a real estate mastermind event. This book changed the way we tracked data, set goals, and understood what challenges lay ahead of us. Gino has a system he calls EOS, or Entrepreneurs Operating System. Although I don't think that EOS totally solves every problem in the complex world of business, it will give you a solid framework to start from.

EOS gave us a few tools that we had not been using or even knew we needed. It gave us the chance every week to solve the biggest problems in one place called the issues list. Anyone on the team can put something on that list, discuss the issue, or propose a solution. We also identified the KPIs (Key Performance Indicators) of the business and started to track them. These included the number of houses we bought, the financial performance of each project, and our overhead cost relative to the profitability of the company. Whether it's EOS or some other system, use something to track what's important and hold yourself and your business accountable for its performance. You will never have your extraordinary life without it.

We learned over time, however, that these systems didn't help us with planning in the business. Initially, we thought that just naming a goal and going for it was the entire planning process, but we were wrong. Over the past year, we've realized that planning involves not just naming what a goal is but actually laying out what could go wrong and what contingencies we needed to plan for. What would plan B be if plan A fails? We needed to have already thought about what issues might come up and what we would do if and when they did.

By learning to plan better and more effectively, we not only made huge strides in accomplishing the goals we laid out but arrived at decisions faster. Planning in detail has forced us to think about the different courses of action we might take. We dial in what we want to accomplish from a big-picture perspective and make it clear who is responsible for visioning, planning, leading, managing, and executing. This level of planning and coordination has fundamentally and positively changed how we operate.

Adjust Course as Necessary and Never Stop Learning

As you clarify what you want in your life and in your business, there will almost certainly be moments you have to adjust. Whether it's the big picture of what you want your life to look like, where you want to live, the size or focus of your business, or the scope of a construction project, things just happen. You change what you want. The only thing you'll know for certain is that the goals you establish and the plans you make will not happen exactly as you thought they would, and that's okay.

Building your extraordinary life doesn't follow a perfectly straight line. At least it hasn't in my life or business, nor in the lives of any of my friends or colleagues. The path you are embarking on will have twists and turns. Challenges will come up that you didn't expect. You will experience triumphs you couldn't have even imagined were possible. All of these experiences are a part of the process and a part of life. Expect them, embrace them, and appreciate whatever happens, not as good or bad, but as a part of your journey creating what you want your life to be.

However successful you are or will become, there are always new challenges you will encounter. Seek out opportunities for learning and growing as a leader, business owner, investor, and human. Learning is a critical component to your success. I'm always looking to learn from others who have created amazing businesses by reading their books and listening to their podcasts. I constantly seek out people who built their lives in the way they wanted. I'm inspired and challenged to refine what I want in my own life just by learning from others who have done the same in their lives.

Focus every single day on what you want to accomplish. Starting each day with a positive mindset. Practice meditation, and give yourself the space to settle your thoughts and be at your best. Take time every day to put your body in motion with a workout, yoga, a walk outside, or smashing the heavy bag. Take what is in your mind, and write down your thoughts and goals—and review them. Make sure your thoughts and actions are in alignment with the vision and goals you've laid out. Execute your plans, and celebrate your wins with something meaningful. Put in place a system that helps you run your business, track your goals, and hold you and your team accountable for the outcomes. Always seek out opportunities to learn, grow, and build your incredible life to be what you want in every facet.

CHAPTER 13

THE EXTRAORDINARY LIFE

I finally began to consistently experience the life I wanted when I gained clarity and took action in every area of my life. Whatever areas I was unhappy about I dug into what was causing that feeling and made changes. I built an awesome real estate brand and started to have a really positive influence in the real estate community. A thriving business that created financial success. The financial resources to do whatever I wanted. Connection with family, friends, and colleagues. And most importantly, joy in my daily experience. These are the components of my extraordinary life, and I am living them as I write this.

Imagine when you are living your own extraordinary life. The work that you do. The incredible business you have created.

The team you've built who you love, who want to work hard, and who all share the common goal of furthering what the business is creating and achieving. You no longer stress about paying the credit card bill or wondering when you can go on vacation. The actions you take and the experiences you have in your life aren't dictated by your financial capacity. The decisions you make, the place you live, the trips you take, and the things you experience in your life are all solely based on what you want.

When an interesting or incredible opportunity comes up for you, it is your decision whether you take the time or spend your resources on that experience. You decide whether to go on an incredible two-week vacation to the French wine country or buy the amazing boat that's been on your vision board for the last four years. Feel the deep satisfaction and contentment that comes with building your extraordinary life and living it.

There will always be challenges that come up in the business or in life, but you can handle them. You've created an environment where you and the people around you are empowered to work through whatever problems arise and solve them with positivity because you created your business to run that way. You've become more patient, kind, and focused because of the journaling and mindset work that you've done. No issue is too complex to understand, strategize, or plan for; you are able so solve whatever problem arises.

This Is Your Life and Not Anyone Else's

As you build and live your extraordinary life, your friends, family, and others you have contact with will begin to notice. You might start to get comments about how lucky you are. Or questions around what you do for a living. You might even get asked bluntly about how you make so much money or can afford to live where you do. Or how you took another week off for another amazing trip. Prepare yourself for these questions and interactions.

You are not responsible for someone else's life or their happiness. Or the success of their business, or the way they manage their personal finances. All of those responsibilities lie only with that person. But people will try to figure out why you are so happy and how you created the life you built. And you now have the exciting opportunity to share with them how they, too, can create their own extraordinary lives.

The more successful I've become, the less I share publically about my life. When I do choose to share, I try to tell about something hard that I overcame or about a really exciting experience or opportunity or investment I made. I've found these kinds of stories can trigger interesting conversations, awakening curiosity and resolve. I want my life to help inspire others to live their life the way they want to live it.

Regardless of how much you share about your life, do it with positivity and kindness. When you encounter someone who says negative things about you, your life, or anything else, don't take them on. Instead, shower them with the positivity and greatness you've created in your life, and let them feel that power even if they don't or can't reciprocate it. You aren't responsible for their happiness, but you are for your own. Never live in negativity.

Live Into Generosity

Making money and creating your life are momentous things you will accomplish. They will open up countless positive opportunities. You will find real purpose in the work you do and the life you live. You will have control over what you spend your time on and where you invest your money. But the most incredible opportunity will be your ability to help others. You will have the chance and power to not only inspire but to change other people's lives.

Imagine for a moment that by living the life you most deeply want to live, you can inspire many other people to live the life they want. You set the bar for what other people want to become and the way they want to live. The kindness, positivity, and love you bring to every moment and every interaction will set an infinitely higher expectation for what a truly successful person is measured by beyond just wealth and possessions.

When you do choose to help someone, set expectations for each of you from the beginning. What is the amount of time you are willing to spend? What are you asking the other person to do with their time, energy, and actions in return? Too often early on, I would spend time trying to help other people but end up feeling frustrated. I didn't set clear expectations for myself or for what the other person would experience as a result of the help I provided. Don't be afraid to give of your time, but be clear about the desired outcome.

Find opportunities to give not just your time but your financial resources. Our family opened a bank account that we titled "charity account," and we deposit money into it every month. Instead of pondering how much we would give to any cause or awesome opportunity, all we have to do was check how much is in the charity account. This practice of giving with purpose is something we intentionally built into our lives.

You don't have to be wealthy to help, inspire, or change someone's life. You might make a massive impact, for example, by taking a breakfast meeting with someone who wants to tap into your knowledge and experience with a matter you know a lot about. Open your own charity account right now, even if you can only put a few dollars in it. Start the habit of not just building a business and the life you want, but looking for opportunities to give your time and your money to help others.

As you live your life, help inspire others, and give money to causes you find important, don't take yourself too seriously. We are all just people living our lives, searching for what it is that really brings us joy, and trying to figure out how to have more of it. Be yourself and appreciate what you have created in your life. Make the importance of your life clear through the positive impact of your actions.

The more you realize how incredible your life really is, the more space you have to give. This isn't about doing things or helping in a way you don't want to. You can give to someone on your team by helping them to buy their first house. Or help a friend figure out how to pay off their credit card or afford to put their kids through school. Even a conversation that you have with someone in passing can transform their life. Don't discount the incredible impact you can have on everyone around you.

Spend Your Time Doing Amazing Things

An extraordinary life is built not just by doing what you want but by finding and experiencing what excites and challenges you. Take the time to explore current interests or what you may have put off learning. Part of being a No Quitter is realizing that you can learn, grow, and challenge yourself in every part of your life and at any age.

One of my new obsessions and challenges has been learning about the outdoors. Over the past few years I've developed a passion for backpacking, hunting, and fishing. I didn't grow up doing any of these things as a kid, and I certainly didn't appreciate how demanding or enriching they would be. I have experienced immense joy learning new skills and spending time in awesome landscapes like the mountains of Nevada, the rivers of Montana, and all of the other incredible places I've been.

Learning how to traverse a snow-covered mountain with a fifty-pound pack on my back was far more physically difficult than I imagined. Confidently threading a fishing line on a fishing rod and then tying a hook onto it took far more effort and practice than I expected. I nearly crashed our new pontoon boat, with friends on board, against the side of a dock while learning to drive it. I've also walked completely drenched with a trash bag over my head in the middle of a rainstorm on the side of a mountain five miles off the road after not bringing proper rain gear. Learning moments make incredible stories and force us to grow and evolve as people.

You don't need to freeze for days at a time on the side of a mountain to live an amazing life. But you do need to choose experiences, hobbies, and challenges to pursue. What do you want to experience? You are building your incredible life to be able to do whatever it is you want with your time. Discover and go after your passions using the same enthusiasm, determination, and effort you applied in building your extraordinary business.

I love having a wide variety of hobbies. I regularly play golf, train for Jiu Jitsu, hunt, fish, collect watches, play multiple instruments, and constantly search out new books and podcasts to learn from. I want to fill my life with amazing experiences, learn incredible skills, and continually grow into the strong, kind, thoughtful person I want to be.

Whatever you choose to learn and spend your time doing is totally up to you, but make the space in your day to enjoy what you decide on. Give yourself the time and grace to learn, and know that just like anything else in life, you will have to spend considerable time working at something to be awesome at it or even capable.

Always Challenge Yourself

As I shared earlier, I recently had the wonderful opportunity to go to the salt flats of Utah to learn to power paraglide. To fly with this thing, you essentially strap a lawnmower with a propeller to your back, then run like a maniac through a field to launch yourself into the air. It is insanely mentally and physically challenging. I learned a lot about my fears, my physical and mental strength, and my willingness to persevere by trying to fly.

I shared on my social media channels the first few times I took off and landed. Most people thought it looked either really awesome or really crazy; I think both assessments are right. What I didn't share was how incredibly difficult it was for me to learn how to take off. All the rest of the skills involved—kiting, bringing the wing overhead, and running with the motor on my back—came easily for me. But when it was time to actually fly, I was the last person in the group to get into the air.

Twice in a row, I got the massive multicolored wing over my head, held the throttle down in my hand, and started running hard, but ended up falling face-first into the dirt. The impact created a cloud of dust that looked like a bomb went off. It challenged every part of me, mentally and physically, to put that motor back on my back, lift the wing, and try again.

Finally, after asking the instructors and fellow participants a lot of questions, it became clear what the real problem was. Once I'd started to run with the wing over my head and switched the motor to full throttle, I needed to pull down on the brakes of the wing. If you don't do that, there isn't enough lift, so you fall down. On my third attempt, I got the wing over my head, hit the throttle, pulled down on the break, and finally experienced flying for the first time. What a surreal feeling I had as I climbed several hundred feet suspended in the air. Even though I'd had a lot of difficulties, I hadn't quit. I worked to understand what the problem was until I got it right.

Fall in Love with Learning

I spend a lot of time every day in the headspace of learning and growing. If I neglect time learning, my life doesn't feel as full or as focused. Listening to books and podcasts constantly challenges me in every area of my life and business. It gives me new ideas to think about and new hobbies I can dig more deeply into. Constant learning is a necessary investment in building your extraordinary life. Spend your time willingly and routinely seeking knowledge and applying it in your life.

Getting into golf has been both an incredible blessing and a daunting challenge. I love the scenic beauty of a well-manicured course and hitting balls for practice at the driving range. Each week, I hit hundreds of golf balls, but I have a very long way to go to be a great golfer. But that's okay, because I love the challenge of becoming a great player and playing a sport I can do for the rest of my life. For me, it's worth the effort and time.

Getting into anything new doesn't mean you have to be great at it right away. You may never be great at it. But welcome the learning, being challenged, and enjoying what you are doing. I felt like I was literally going to throw up the first time I sparred in the MMA gym with my coach. The feeling of him punching me in the body was nauseating, and the pain of being kicked was like absorbing a baseball bat to the legs. For months, every time I sparred, I was terrified, barely able to breathe, and utterly exhausted.

However, eventually, I was regularly sparring with many professional fighters and was no longer afraid of contact. I had mental clarity as the rounds went on and got into awesome shape training and sparring for many hours every week. Some experiences you go after might literally or metaphorically end up with you getting punched in the face. But embrace whatever you have chosen to spend your time on with all that you have mentally, physically, and emotionally. Get out of it all you can. You will be a better, stronger, more confident person not just when doing that activity but in all areas of your life.

Hunting and fishing expeditions have brought me outdoors to some of the highest, most remote, most beautiful, and most dangerous places and conditions in North America. I have sat quietly on snow-covered mountains in subfreezing conditions and questioned my sanity. What was I doing there? But looking back, I see I was learning patience, persistence, and the willingness to do what it takes. Every opportunity or challenge you put yourself in the middle of not only helps you grow in that moment, but also offers lessons you can apply to everything else you do.

Most of all, every experience, challenge, and pursuit in my life has made me a better human. I've learned about who I am and want to be—a successful business partner, a caring husband, and a kind, loving father. These experiences help me be a better friend, too, and a generally more empathetic person. I remain open to even more new and interesting opportunities, and I am profoundly thankful for my life. I want to be a go-giver, giving my time, my understanding, and my financial resources. Life becomes so simple when we realize that everything we do is about finding our purpose, experiencing love, and enjoying our life.

Prepare for Your Incredible Life-Changing Journey

When I read books that inspire me or learn something new that I expect to be transformational, I have a very hard time being patient and waiting to see the actual change happen. Just like the examples of learning to fly a paraglider or sparring in mixed martial arts, all skills take time and practice to develop, especially to the point where you can execute them consistently at a high level. If you are like me, you will want this incredible business and your incredible life to happen right now. But don't let short-term setbacks cloud your focus, your positivity, or the end result you are creating. Your extraordinary life is going to take time to build, and it will be worth every effort and challenge you encounter while creating it.

Working a job you don't like and having experiences that aren't what you want isn't the life you were meant to live. You can create whatever life you want by finding your why or purpose for being, a reason that extends beyond yourself. Create a vision for what your life looks like, including how you will spend your time, the business you will build, and the extraordinary experiences you will enjoy. You have the power to transform your life into whatever you want it to be.

Don't allow yourself to get sucked into get rich schemes or thinking that your goal is just becoming famous and having a bunch of followers on Instagram. Instead of focusing on the everyday hustle and grind, focus on what you actually want to experience in your life. Live in the power of what you want your life to look like. Build your business around it. You will not experience real success without maintaining a high level of focus and purposefulness in every area of your life. The business you create should be built to serve you.

Develop and maintain a No Quitters' mindset. No matter what you encounter, you have the ability and capacity to solve the problem. Accept that hard situations are going to come up and appreciate and learn from them. They will help you understand what you are doing well and areas where you need to improve, reassess, or adjust. Live in a mindset of abundance, not fear or frustration over someone else's success. Anyone can create the life they want to live. Put only positive energy into the world for others as you are creating your own. You are solely responsible for creating, building, and living your incredible life.

With clear focus, lay out the plan of the business so that it will be the financial engine of your life. Your business is meant to serve you, so create it in a way that gives you the life and experience you want. Remember the size of your portfolio or the amount of money you make isn't a direct reflection of your success. You define what your incredible life consists of.

There are all kinds of ways to invest in real estate, and you can choose what attracts you or fits your goals. Whether you decide on growing a real estate portfolio, wholesaling properties to other investors, or flipping hundreds of homes a year, you can get incredible financial results. Think about the lifestyle you want to live. How many hours do you want to spend working within the business? What are the responsibilities and roles you will hold within your organization? Let your answers drive how you build your business and you will have fulfilling work that produces the financial result you desire.

As you create your business, hold onto the driving why of your life. It will remind you that you have a purpose in life beyond just making money, like helping other people. Your why goes beyond just you. It includes the incredible impact your decisions, business, and life will have on those around you, today and far into the future.

Build incredible relationships and surround yourself with positive people who want you to be successful. Find mentors and coaches who can help you see issues or work through challenges that you have not yet encountered or solved. I would not be anywhere close to where I am in my life without so many incredible people who have helped and mentored me on my real estate journey.

All this time, effort, struggle, and perseverance will pay off. You can and will create the most incredible life you can imagine and live it every day. Anytime you are struggling and wonder if your effort is worth it, come back to the vision you've laid out and the impact your why will have not just on you but on the world. Creating your extraordinary life won't just change your life, but the lives of so many others around you, including people you may never even meet. Your life will be the inspiration and maybe even the blueprint for someone else to change their life.

Prepare yourself to be successful. Live in the incredible place you want to call home and drive whatever car you want to drive (even if it's not a Porsche, though you will never convince me they aren't the coolest, sexiest, and most amazing cars ever made). You will get to spend your time doing what you want. The decisions you make and the experiences you have won't be based on whether you have the time or money to do them, but if they are what you want to spend your time doing.

You can envision, build, and live whatever life you want. There is nothing keeping you from success. No obstacles will block you from accomplishing your goal. When you encounter struggles, start by clearing your mind, understanding the real issues, and then addressing them head-on. The goals you set and the effective action you take are the only limiting factors of your success.

Be clear on what your extraordinary life is, have conviction in your plan, and go build it.

TAKE MASSIVE ACTION
AND CONNECT WITH ME

Whenever you find yourself struggling, remember that you have an entire community to support you in seeking success. Connect with thousands of other investors looking to create their own extraordinary lives on our online forums and at www.noquittersguide.com. And please email (nathan@noquittersguide.com) to share your extraordinary life with me or share with us on Facebook or Instagram. I love hearing what you have created in your own life, so thanks for including me.

Part of my mission in life is not just to inspire you but for you to have real change in your life and experience it the way you want. I believe you can and will be able to live whatever life you want. And I deeply care that you take what you've learned from this book and put it into action. Learning is only as impactful as the actions you take that stem from the lessons you learn.

Come hang out with other entrepreneurs, dreamers, and world-changers at www.noquittersguide.com. I wanted to create a place for you to be inspired, hear stories, and connect with other No Quitters. Learning and growing are absolutely critical and have been one of the main keys to my success, so this website is where you can continue to learn and develop. When you are ready, you will find that our simple online course was built as an incredible resource to help you continue on your path creating and building your extraordinary life. You can take action and be successful without the course, but it is there to help you jumpstart your journey, build your why, focus your effort, and crush your goals.

Above all, I want to end with gratitude. The dream of writing this book has been heavy on me for several years. I've wanted to have a massive impact on your life and to give you not just an idea of what life could look like but a blueprint for you to create an extraordinary life for yourself. Thank you for spending your precious time with me, reading the words on these pages. I've written them with my own hands and pored over them, trying to shape them into the clearest guidance for you. My prayer, my hope, and my goal for this book is that you will be inspired and have the belief in yourself to take action and change your life forever.

It's time now. That's enough reading, dreaming, and learning inside the walls of these chapters. Take your pen and paper out. Open up the pages of your journal. And do the work ahead of you. Create an incredible vision of your life based on the why that drives you. Cultivate an unshakable positive mindset. Whatever you encounter or whatever problem you have to solve, you will figure out the answer and solve it.

Go build your extraordinary life and live it.

ACKNOWLEDGMENTS

I wrote this book with all the love and care I have because I wanted to help you, the reader, create a vision for your life and an actual plan to manifest it. Use the book as a roadmap to building the extraordinary business and life you want. I hope it will inspire every dreamer who finds their way to its pages. I see you! Just know, I am here celebrating you and cheering you on, wherever you and I are in the world. Believe in your ability to succeed. Promise to lay out your vision, create your plan, and NO QUITTING until you have accomplished the goals you set. Remember, no matter where you are in life, that isn't where you have to end up.

I wouldn't have created my own extraordinary life or mul-timillion-dollar real estate business without so many incredible people who have positively impacted my life and helped me along the way. I'm so grateful for each and every one of you.

There are entirely too many people to mention, so please forgive me if I haven't mentioned you by name. I am deeply appreciative of all the help, guidance, coaching, and mentoring you have endlessly and graciously shared with me over the last decade plus.

Thank you to my first real estate mentor, Rob, who laid out what a robust and successful real estate business looks like. You forever changed my life. Gary, my real estate coach and dear friend, for setting the example of what a well-run business really looks like. To Larry, Annie, and the entire team for helping us work through a massively challenging and pivotal moment in our company. David, one of my closest friends and business partner, I appreciate you more than words can express.

This book simply would not have come together in the way that it did without the brilliance and guidance of Ashley, my book coach. Her endless patience and firm confidence in this book could not have made a bigger impact. And to Katherine, my editor, who slaved over every comma, word, and sentence, I can't thank you enough. Thanks to David and the whole Morgan James team for believing in my book and guiding it through publication.

Brandon Turner! I love you man. And I appreciate all the areas of your life you are crushing from podcasting, writing numerous incredible real estate books, to now launching and growing your fund in such a short time. Thank you for inspiring me. Leading and living into your own extraordinary life.

And, to my beautiful family: Stacy, Collin, and Grace. I love you all very much. Thank you for the support, inspiration, quiet space to write, endless cups of tea while writing, and just the opportunity to write this book. I'm on fire to have an impact on the lives of people who read it. None of this would be possible without the lessons, struggles, experiences, and life we have experienced together.

I've wanted to write this book for so many years. I really can't believe this is real. What an extraordinary life this is.

—Nathan

ABOUT THE AUTHOR

Nathan Brooks, CEO, Bridge Turnkey Investments

Nathan Brooks is the cofounder and CEO of Bridge Turnkey Investments, a home builder in the Kansas City metro area, poised to construct sixty new homes in its first few years of operation. Prior to building homes, Nathan led Bridge as one of the top-producing turnkey rental providers in the nation, adding over $45 million in value to his clients' portfolios in just a few short years.

Having invested in real estate since 2007, Nathan is an accomplished investor and a sought-after speaker, writer, and real estate coach. He regularly produces educational content to fuel his passion for helping other people learn about and find success in real estate investing. To this end, he recently wrote his first book, *The No Quitters' Guide to Crushing Real Estate Investing and Living an Extraordinary Life*, which has already received accolades from heavy hitters in the industry like Bigger Pockets' Brandon Turner.

Nathan is a passionate leader, well-respected investor, and friend to everyone he meets. He currently lives in Kansas City on his 11-acre property with his wife and two beautiful children, where he enjoys the outdoors, training in MMA, playing golf, hunting, and finding new ways to challenge himself.

A free ebook edition is available with the purchase of this book.

To claim your free ebook edition:

1. Visit MorganJamesBOGO.com
2. Sign your name CLEARLY in the space
3. Complete the form and submit a photo of the entire copyright page
4. You or your friend can download the ebook to your preferred device

A **FREE** ebook edition is available for you or a friend with the purchase of this print book.

CLEARLY SIGN YOUR NAME ABOVE

Instructions to claim your free ebook edition:
1. Visit MorganJamesBOGO.com
2. Sign your name CLEARLY in the space above
3. Complete the form and submit a photo of this entire page
4. You or your friend can download the ebook to your preferred device

Print & Digital Together Forever.

Snap a photo   Free ebook   Read anywhere